E. A. Wallis Budge

The History of Esarhaddon, Son of Sennacherib, King of Assyria, B. C. 681-688

Tr. from the cuneiform inscriptions upon cylinders and tablets in the British museum collection, together with original texts; a grammatical analysis of each word

E. A. Wallis Budge

The History of Esarhaddon, Son of Sennacherib, King of Assyria, B. C. 681-688
Tr. from the cuneiform inscriptions upon cylinders and tablets in the British museum collection, together with original texts; a grammatical analysis of each word

ISBN/EAN: 9783337245801

Printed in Europe, USA, Canada, Australia, Japan

Cover: Foto ©ninafisch / pixelio.de

More available books at **www.hansebooks.com**

TRÜBNER'S

ORIENTAL SERIES

THE

HISTORY OF ESARHADDON

(*SON OF SENNACHERIB*)

KING OF ASSYRIA, B.C. 681—668

Translated from the Cuneiform Inscriptions upon Cylinders and Tablets in the British Museum Collection

TOGETHER WITH

Original Texts

A GRAMMATICAL ANALYSIS OF EACH WORD, EXPLANATIONS OF THE IDEOGRAPHS BY EXTRACTS FROM THE BI-LINGUAL SYLLABARIES, AND LIST OF EPONYMS, ETC.

BY

ERNEST A. BUDGE, M.R.A.S.

MEMBER OF THE SOCIETY OF BIBLICAL ARCHÆOLOGY

LONDON

TRÜBNER & CO., LUDGATE HILL

1880

This Book is Dedicated

TO

HIS TRUSTY FRIEND AND TEACHER,

THE REV. A. H. SAYCE, M.A.

Deputy Professor of Comparative Philology, Oxford, &c. &c. &c.

BY THE AUTHOR,

IN GRATEFUL REMEMBRANCE OF MANY YEARS' VALUABLE TUITION.

PREFACE.

THE histories of Sennacherib and Assur-bani-pal, kings of Assyria, have already been written by the late Mr. George Smith. Sennacherib ruled over Assyria from B.C. 705 to B.C. 681; Assur-bani-pal from B.C. 668 to B.C. 626. But from B.C. 681 to B.C. 668 a king called Esarhaddon reigned, and the annals of this king have been translated to form the present history. Esarhaddon was the son of Sennacherib, and father of Assur-bani-pal. Thus we have the history of father, son, and grandson; consequently, a fair knowledge of the warlike expeditions which were undertaken, and what countries were subdued by the Assyrians, between the years B.C. 705 and B.C. 626. Sennacherib, Esarhaddon and Assur-bani-pal were certainly three of the greatest kings that ever ruled over Assyria. Their reigns, taken together, cover nearly eighty years; but an exact idea of the influence that this family had upon Assyria can only be made out clearly from the records and documents which they themselves caused to be written. Sennacherib was the true type of the Oriental conqueror—delighting in war for its own sake, proud, cruel, and fond of power. The Bible preserves for us a speech of the Rabshakeh[1]

[1] This is the Accadian , D.P., RAB-SAK, borrowed by the Hebrews under the form רַבְשָׁקֵה; *rab* is the Semitic equivalent of the Accadian , GAL, "great."

of Sennacherib, so well known on account of the boastfulness and pride so vividly portrayed in every word. The commencement, Thus saith "the great king, the King of Assyria,"[1] is the oft-repeated formula beginning all the inscriptions of this monarch. We can quite understand such a king asking, "Where are the gods of Hamath and of Arpad? who are they among all the gods of the countries, that the Lord should deliver Jerusalem out of mine hand?" for he frequently boasts, "the gods of his country I carried off, I spoiled."

The sway of Esarhaddon was, however, milder, and although he warred as much as "the king his father, who went before," yet he exhibits many signs of gentleness, and it is evident that he tried to pacify all those subjects that successful warfare had allowed him to conquer. It must be clear to all how valuable are the cuneiform inscriptions that give us the history of this monarch. The Bible mentions him but three times by name;[2] he is alluded to once.[3]

Esarhaddon's son, Assur-bani-pal, was the literary king *par excellence*, and he records of himself that "Nebo and Tasmit gave him broad ears, and his seeing eyes regarded the engraved characters of the tablets, the secrets of Nebo, the literature of the library, as much as is suitable, on tablets I wrote, I engraved, I explained, and for the inspection of my subjects in the midst of my palace I placed" (*W.A.I.*, iv. pl. 55).

The following is his full and interesting account of his subjection of Tirhakah, King of Egypt and Cush, translated from the large decagon cylinder containing the "Annals of Assur-

1 

2 2 Kings xix. 37; Isaiah xxxvii. 38; Ezra iv. 2.

3 2 Chron. xxxiii. 11.

banipal," recently brought from the East, and bearing the number R^{M} 1 in the British Museum collection :—

1 In my first expedition to the land of Māgan and Melukh-kha, then I went.
2 Tirhakah, King of Egypt and Cush,
3 of whom Esarhaddon, King of Assyria, the father, my begetter,
4 his overthrow had accomplished, and had ruled over his land, then he, Tirhakah,
5 the power of Assur (and) Istar, the great gods, my lords, despised, and
6 he trusted to his own might. Against the kings,
7 prefects, which within Egypt, the father, my begetter, had appointed
8 to slay, plunder, and capture Egypt, he came
9 against them, he entered and dwelt within Memphis,
10 the city which the father, my begetter, had captured, and to the border of Assyria had added it.
11 I was walking within Nineveh, (when) one came and
12 repeated to me concerning these deeds.
13 My heart groaned and was smitten down my liver.
14 I lifted up my two hands; I besought Assur and Istar, the holy one.
15 (Then) I assembled my powerful forces, (with) which Assur and Istar
16 had filled my two hands. Against the lands of Egypt and Cush
17 I set straight the expedition. . . . .
27 Tirhakah, King of Egypt and Cush, within Memphis,
28 of the march of my expedition heard, and to make battle; (his) weapons
29 and army {against / before} me he assembled, (with) his soldiers.
23 In the service of Assur, Bel, the great gods, my lords,
24 the marchers before me in a great field battle, I accomplished the overthrow of his army.

25 Tirhakah, within Memphis, heard of the defeat of his army.
26 the terror of Assur and Istar overwhelmed him, and he went backward,
27 the fear (approach) of my lordship covered him.
28 The city Memphis he turned from, and for the saving of his life
29 he fled to the midst of Thebes.
30 That city I captured, my army I caused to enter and to dwell within it.

Col. 2.

20 Tirhakah fled from his locality, (but) the fire of the weapon of Assur, my lord,
21 overwhelmed him, and he went to his dark destiny.

His grandest work was the institution of the great library of clay tablets at Koyunjik.

And now as regards the texts, translations and notes that are contained in this book. I have used all the principal historical texts, and every line of these has been carefully compared with the original clay tablets and cylinders in the British Museum. But it cannot be expected that every notice concerning Esarhaddon which may be found upon contract or other tablets will be given in so small a book.

In the first place, it would necessitate a strict and careful examination of every tablet and tablet-fragment in the British Museum collection, which alone would require many many months to be devoted entirely to the purpose—no small task either, as any will see who knows the nature of the writing on the tablets.

Secondly, when done, the chances are that it would place the book entirely out of the reach of commercial enterprise.

These two reasons, taken together, will account for the omission of the text and translation of a tablet containing "Addresses to Esarhaddon,"[1] and also of another containing an account of Esarhaddon's buildings, and numbered K 3053.

The translations are as literal as possible, and all added words are enclosed in brackets. Parts of the texts relating the history of Esarhaddon have been translated before by my friend Dr. Julius Oppert, Professor of Arabic in the University of France,[2] the profound scholar and earliest pioneer of Assyrian in France.

The grammatical analysis has been thrown into a vocabulary arranged according to the order of the English alphabet. The object has been to make the words easily accessible and useful. Wherever I have known a Semitic equivalent for the Assyrian word it has been given, but words properly Syriac have been turned into Hebrew letters. The sense of some of the words is only known from the context, and of course there are some the meaning of which I do not know at all.

Here I take the opportunity of expressing my great obligations to the Rev. A. H. Sayce, M.A., for several years past my kind friend and teacher. It is to him that I am indebted for anything I may know of Assyrian. The whole of the MS. for this book was read by him before it went to press, and it owes much to his scholarly and accurately critical eye.

My thanks are also due to Mr. Pinches for copies of texts and verifications of existing copies.

[1] The text is printed in *W.A.I.*, iv. 68, and translated in the *Records of the Past*, vol. xi.

[2] See *Expédition Scientifique en Mésopotamie éxécutée par ordre du Gouvernement de* 1851 *à* 1854. Par MM. F. Fresnel, F. Thomas et J. Oppert. Paris, 1857-64.

New advances are made in Assyrian with every new tablet that is found. Old readings are corrected, new words are found, and what is almost unintelligible to-day becomes quite clear to-morrow. With such progress going on, no book can be perfect; and as for this, I feel that

[1] אמנם השניתי כי אין אנוש שלא יחטא הלא אתי תלין משונתי: אחלי
שגיאות מי יבין וידעם. יתקין לפי שכלו עוות שגיאותי:

"Truly I have committed errors, for there is no man who does not err; so that my error cleaves to me. I pray, therefore, that whoever understands and knows them, may correct my errors according to his wisdom."

E. A. BUDGE.

CHRIST'S COLLEGE, CAMBRIDGE,
October, 1880.

[1] I quote from Levita, *Massoreth Ha-massoreth*, p. 268, by Dr. Ginsburg. Longmans. 1867.

CONTENTS.

ERRATA.

Page 3, line 1, instead of	ideograph	read ideographs.
„ 7, „ 7, „	Saulmugina	„ Samullu-suma-ucin; and wherever it occurs.
„ 22, „ 13, „		„ 
„ 22, „ 13, „		„ 
„ 24, „ 19, „		„ 
„ 32, „ 9, „		„ 
„ 36, „ 25, „		„ 
„ 36, „ 36, „		„ 
„ 38, „ 41, „		„ 
„ 55, „ 56, „	ARBA	„ IRBA
„ 68, „ 56, „	ina-khats-zu-va	„ im-khats-zu-va
„ 78, „ 10, „		„ 
„ 80, „ 19, „		„ 
„ 85, „ 47, „	śi-gar-si-ui	„ śi-gar-si-in
„ 92, „ 36, „		„ 
„ 93, *note*, l. 8, „	Tirpanituv	„ Tsarpanituv
„ 104, „ 17, „		„ 
„ 104, „ 18, „		„ 

„ 109. Concerning the history of Tirhakah, see a paper by Dr. Birch which will appear in the *Trans. Soc. Bib. Arch.*, vol. vii. part 2.

ADDENDA.

I. While *The History of Esarhaddon* was passing through the press Dr. Schrader's new work, *Zur Kritik der Inschriften Tiglath-Pileser's II. des Asarhaddon und des Asurbanipal,* appeared. On pages 34 and 35 he identifies some of the towns and countries mentioned by Esarhaddon, and printed on pages 103–107 of this book. Thus, concerning "'Samsimuruna" he says, "Eine Stadt des Namens Samsimurun ist bis jetzt in Palästina-Phönicien überhaupt nicht nachzuweisen." He points out (as I have also done on page 107 of *The History of Esarhaddon*) that the hitherto accepted reading of "Amtikhadatsti" is wrong, and should be "Karti-khadatsti," "Newstadt," קרת חדשת (Assyrisch regelrecht חדסת ק״), "bedeutet und einfach ein cyprisches Καρχηδὼν = Karthago ist." Dr. Schrader likewise points out that in Esarhaddon's List of Kings the King of Arvad is called, "Matanbaal (מַתַּנְבַּעַל), but in Assurbanipal's list "Yacinlu" (יכנאל); also the name of the King of Beth-Ammon in the former list is "Puduilu (פְּדָהְאֵל), but in the latter Amminadbi, Heb. עַמִּינָדָב; and thinks "dass wir es bei dieser zweiten Liste nichts weniger als mit einer gedankenlosen oder gar frivol-leichtsinnigen Reproducirung der früheren des Asarhaddon zu thun haben." Also, see "Zusätze," page 36 of Dr. Schrader's book, for the opinion of Professor R. A. Lepsius, of Jena, concerning the town of Lidir, situated in Cyprus.

II. In the "Vocabulary" all parts of the verb "suzubu" have been compared with the Hebrew √ עזב. But I believe its correct equivalent to be found in the Chaldee שֵׁיזִיב or שֵׁיזֵב, "to save," "to deliver;" Syriac שוזב. Compare Targum on Isaiah xx. 6, נַפְשְׁהוֹן לָא שֵׁיזִיבוּ, "themselves they deliver (save) not;" ומן רשיעא דמשתוזב, "and who is the wicked man that shall be saved" (Ephraem, "Carmina," Opp. iii. p. 635; Rödiger, Chrestomathy, p. 79); איכנא דאשוזב לעלמא, "that I shall save the world" (John xii. 47). In the expression, "ana suzub napsate su," "for the saving of his life," I would compare the word "suzub" with Chaldee שֵׁיזָבָא, or Rabbinic שֵׁיזְבָא, "deliverance, escape."

III. Ittagil, from √ "dagalu." With this compare Chaldee תְּכַל, "fidere, confidere, fiduciam ponere vel collocare;" and see Psalm ix. 11, where וְיִבְטְחוּ is translated by one MS. וְיִתְכְּלוּן, "and they trusted."

Rm 1, col. 1, lines 8, 9.

 (*W.A.I.*, iv. 68, 52–53.)

וישב סנחריב מלך־אשור וישב בנינוה׃
ויהי הוא משתחוה בית נסרך אלהיו
ואדרמלך ושראצר בניו הכהו בחרב
והמה נמלטו ארץ אררט וימלך
אסר־חדו בנו תחתיו׃

(Isai. xxxvii. 37, 38.)

אסר חדון מלך אשור . בנו של סנחרב שלאחר סנחרב

(Rashi on Ezra iv. 2.)

כי סנחרב שגלה את ישראל הומת ע״י בניו ומלך אסר חדון בנו תחתיו

(מצודת דוד on Ezra iv. 2.)

THE GENEALOGY AND ACCESSION OF ESARHADDON, AND PRINCIPAL EVENTS OF HIS REIGN.

Esarhaddon was the son of Sennacherib, king of Assyria, B.C. 705–681. The Sin-akhi-irib of the cuneiform inscriptions is the—

סַנְחֵרִיב of the Bible;
LXX. Σενναχηρίμ, or Σενναχηρείμ;
Josephus, Σενναχήριβος;
Herodotus, Σαναχάριβος.

The sons of Sennacherib were—

1 Sharesar, Biblical שַׂרְאֶצֶר (Nergal-sarra-yutsur);
2 Adrammelech, ,, אַדְרַמֶּלֶךְ;
3 Esarhaddon, ,, אֵסַר־חַדּוֹן,
written Ἀσορδάν and Σαχερδονός, Berosus and LXX.;
,, Ἀσαρίδανος, Ptolemy;
,, Ἀσαράδαν, Ezra;
,, Σαχερδών, Codex Alex.
,, Ἀχειρδωνός, Compl.

The account of the death of Sennacherib is told us by the Bible, and very briefly, for we read (2 Kings xix. 37): "And it came to pass as he (Sennacherib) was worshipping in the house of Nisroch his god, that Adrammelech and Shareser his sons smote him with the sword; and they escaped into the land of Armenia. And Esarhaddon his son reigned in his stead."[1]

Josephus says (*Ant.*, x. 1, sec. 5) that Sennacherib was buried "in his own temple called Araske" ('εν τῷ ἰδίῳ ναῷ 'Αράσκῃ λεγομένῳ).

It has been generally thought that Esarhaddon was Sennacherib's eldest son, and this seems to have been the idea of Polyhistor, who made Sennacherib place a son, *Asordanes*, on the throne of Babylon during his own lifetime (Ap. Euseb., *Chron.*, Can. i. 5).[2] The testimony of a small tablet (*W.A.I.*, iii., 16) supports this view.

It has been aptly called the "Will of Sennacherib."[3] It reads—

> "I, Sennacherib, king of multitudes, king of Assyria,
> have given chains of gold, etc., to
> Esarhaddon, my son, who was afterwards named
> Assur-ebil-mucin-pal,
>
> 
>
> according to my wish."

The name of Esarhaddon is written in the following ways—

D.P. Assur - akha - IDIN - na.—i. 49, 1.

D.P. Assur-akha-idinna.—i. 48, 2, 1.

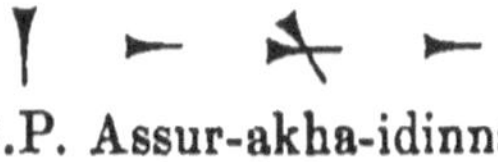

D.P. Assur-akha-idinna.—i. 48, 5, 1.

It means "Assur gave a brother."

[1] These events are mentioned, with additions, by Berosus (Berosus and Abydenus ap. Eusebius, *Chron. Armen*, ed. Aucher, vol. i. pp. 42, 43); Gesenius, *Theasaurus*, p. 962.

[2] Smith's *Dict. of Bible*, large edition.

[3] *Records of the Past*, vol. i. p. 136.

The syllabaries explain the ideograph employed in the name thus:—

 =  i-luv. Heb. אֵל, ii. 31, 27.

 = Assuru. Heb. אַשּׁוּר, Sayce, *Syl.*, 414.

 =  a-khu. Heb. אָח, ii. 2, 276.

 =  na-da-nu. Heb. נָתַן, iii. 70, 77.

 =  a-khu. Sayce, *Syl.*, 13.

 =  na-da-nu. Sayce, *Syl.* 1.

The character  is a variant form for , Assur. It is found on an altar slab of Assur-natsir-pal (*Trans. Soc. Bib. Arch.*, vol. vii.).

Esarhaddon began to reign B.C. 681, and he reigned until B.C. 668. His brothers Adrammelech and Sharesser attempted to obtain the throne, but Esarhaddon drew up his army, and, marching against them, gained a complete victory at Khanirabbat, a district on the Upper Euphrates. According to some, Adrammelech was killed in battle; according to others, he escaped with his brother and took refuge in Armenia. According to local tradition, the king of Armenia received the vanquished with great kindness, and gave them land to dwell in.[1]

A tablet, containing "addresses" to Esarhaddon, was probably drawn up at the time when Esarhaddon was preparing to fight against his brothers. Column II. speaks thus (*W.A.I.* iv. 68):—

14 Fear not, Oh Esarhaddon,
15 I (am) Bel, thy strength.
16 & 17 I will ease the supports of thy heart.
18 Respect, as for thy mother,
19 Thou hast caused to be shown to me.
20 (Each) of the sixty great gods, my strong ones,
21 Will guide thee with his life——
25 Upon mankind trust not, (but)

[1] Maspero, *Histoire Ancienne*, p. 422. Moses of Khorene, *History of Armenia*, I., i. p. 22.

26 Bend thine eyes
27 Upon me—trust to me! (for)
28 I am Istar of Arbela.

After the battle (B.C. 680), Esarhaddon marched into Nineveh. But about this time Nabu-zir-napisti-eser, son of Merodach-Baladan, an old enemy of Assyria, raised an army and went to attack the city of Ur, whose eponym's name was Nin-gal-iddina (?). He was successful in his siege, and captured the city. Esarhaddon sent out his officers, and Nabu-zir-napisti-esir, knowing this, fled to Elam, asking protection from Umman-aldas, king of that country. But this was refused; and in col. 2, lines 33 and 34, we read that "he had trusted to the king of Elam, who had not caused his life to be spared." Nahid-Marduk, another son of Merodach-Baladan, hearing of the death of his brother, came to Nineveh and sought alliance with Esarhaddon, who received him graciously, and gave him the sea-coast to rule over.

Another revolt in Syria now claimed the attention of the Assyrian king. Abdi-milcutti, king of the city of Zidon, had made alliance with 'Sānduarri, king of Cundi and 'Sizū. Esarhaddon marched against Zidon, besieged and captured it. He cut off the heads of Abdi-milcutti and 'Sānduarri, and, hanging them upon the necks of their great men, exhibited them in the wide spaces (Rehoboth) in Nineveh.

All Palestine and the neighbouring regions now submitted to Esarhaddon—viz., twelve districts in Palestine, and ten in Cyprus. Each king sent presents.

At this time, also, he captured the city of Arzani, perhaps a city of Egypt.

Esarhaddon's next expedition was against the Gimirrai, or Kimmerians, whose king was called Teuspa. He conquered them, and, at the same time, the inhabitants of Cilicia and Dūha submitted.

Soon after this, Esarhaddon attacked the Mannai, but in this attempt he appears not to have been quite as successful. However, five Median chiefs came to Nineveh and submitted to Esarhaddon.

Esarhaddon now attempted the conquest of Arabia. Many of the Assyrian kings before Esarhaddon had made some conquests in the land of Edom. But he went farther, and reached two cities, called Bāzu and Khazu (the Biblical Huz and Buz), and conquered eight kings and queens. The journey, however, was very difficult, and little more is said about it.

A king, called Lailie, asked that the gods which Esarhaddon had captured from him might be restored. His request was granted, and Esarhaddon says—"I spoke to him of brotherhood, and entrusted to him the sovereignty of the districts of Bāzu."

Esarhaddon being master of Arabia, Syria, Media, and the other countries which had rebelled against him, was now troubled by Egypt. Before the reign of Esarhaddon, an Ethiopian, called Sabaka, had conquered Egypt. He died, and Sabatok, his successor, made good his cause, and was recognised as king.[1] But now Tirhakah fought Sabatok, who was vanquished, taken prisoner, and put to death.[2]

Tirhakah had been a stubborn and rebellious enemy against Sennacherib, the father of Esarhaddon. It was his army that had opposed Sennacherib at the time of the overthrow of the Assyrian army. Tirhakah, having reigned about twenty years, considered himself well established on the Egyptian throne, so he made an alliance with Bāhlu, king of Tyre, and as it is said—

> "The yoke of Assur, my lord, they despised; they were insolent and rebellious."

"Esarhaddon had entered into a convention with Bahal, by which, in return for services rendered by the Tyrians, the Assyrian monarch ceded to the king of Tyre a considerable portion of the coast of Palestine, including Accho, Dor, and all the northern coast of the Philistines, with the cities and Gebal, and Lebanon, and the cities in the mountains behind Tyre." [3]

This very serious rebellion aroused Esarhaddon and brought him and his army against the rebels. He started from the

[1] Oppert, *Mémoire sur les Rapports de l'Egypte et de l'Assyrie*, p. 14.

[2] *Manetho*, edited Unger, p. 251.

[3] Smith's *Assyria*, p. 34.

city Aphek, and marched as far as Rapikhi (?), a journey of 30 *casbu*, or 210 miles.

The Assyrian army was short of water, and was obliged to drink whatever water could be found, for he says—

"Marsh waters from buckets I caused my army to drink."

He then marched into Egypt, and Tirhakah was beaten.

Esarhaddon next divided Egypt into twenty provinces; all, except two, being governed by Egyptian generals.

The exceptions are:—

Sar-ludari, king of the city of Tsiahnu (Zoan, or Tanis), and Bucur-Ninip, king of the city of Pākhnuti.

Esarhaddon caused to be carved upon the rocks of the Nahr-el-Kelb a long inscription, in which he called himself "King of Egypt, Thebes, and Ethiopia."[1] B.C. 672.

Esarhaddon now began his buildings. He first built "ten fortresses" in Assyria and Accad. He then repaired and enlarged the palace at Nineveh, which had been made for the "custody of the camp-baggage." The twenty-two kings of Syria (for their names see text) brought him materials for his works. He began a palace at Calah, but it was never finished; and he built one for his son, Assur-bani-pal, at Tarbitsi (modern Sheref Khan).

While Esarhaddon was yet king, he set his son Assur-bani-pal upon the throne to reign with him. This is evident from *W.A.I.*, iii. 1, 7, 9, where it is said:—

9 Esarhaddon, king of Assyria, the father, my begetter.
10 The will of Assur and Beltis the gods, his ministers, he exalted.
11 Which (gods) commanded him to establish my kingship.

The inscription then goes on to say that, on the 12th day of May, Esarhaddon gathered together the principal men of the kingdom, and it was decreed that Assur-bani-pal should be made king. This event must have taken place between B.C. 671 and B.C. 668.

[1] Oppert, *Mémoires sur les Rapports de l'Egypte et de l'Assyrie*, pp. 38, 43, 80, et seq.

When Esarhaddon returned to Assyria, Tirhakah raised a large army and went to besiege Memphis. The city fell into his hands after a "murderous siege."[1] The account of his defeat is given by the annals of Assur-bani-pal. Esarhaddon died in the year B.C. 668.

He left one son, Assur-bani-pal, king of Assyria, and another called generally Saulmugina, king of Babylon. Their names are thus written :—

Assur-bani-pal, 

Saulmugina, 

Esarhaddon was truly "the great king," and he adopted the policy of holding court at Nineveh and Babylon. Babylon was the scene of many great battles, and during its existence was fought for oftener than, perhaps, any other city in the Babylonian and Assyrian empires. It was said to have been built in very early times, became capital under Khammuragas, and held this position for 1200 years (*Babylonia*, p. 75). Khammuragas (about B.C. 1700) calls himself "king of Babylon." He built there a temple to Merodach.

It was conquered by Tuculti-Ninip B.C. 1271; by Tiglath-Pileser I. B.C. 1110; by Tiglath-Pileser II. B.C. 731; by Merodach-Baladan B.C. 722; by Sargon B.C. 721; it was sacked and burnt by Sennacherib B.C. 692, but restored by Esarhaddon B.C. 675; captured by Assur-bani-pal B.C. 648, also by Nabu-pal-yutsur B.C. 626, and finally taken by the Medes and Persians B.C. 539.[2]

In his capacity of ruler he was comparatively merciful and kind, for the phrase "riemu arsi-su" (I showed mercy to him) occurs frequently in the inscriptions; also his restoration

[1] Oppert, *Les Sargonides*, p. 57.

[2] For the measurement of its walls, etc.—See Diodorus Siculus, vol. i. pp. 118, 120. Amstelodami, 1746.

to his enemies of the gods which he had captured is probably without equal among the deeds of the mighty kings of Assyria "who went before." Another proof of his generosity to his enemies is shown by the fact of his releasing Manasseh, king of Judah, and restoring to him his kingdom after he had been carried captive to Babylon (2 Chron. xxxiii. 11). He extended the Assyrian empire by the conquests of Arabia and Egypt, and does not appear to have taken delight in warlike expeditions for their own sake, but only undertook them when necessity required for the submission of his enemies.

LIST OF TEXTS USED OR CONSULTED FOR THIS BOOK.

The brick legends lithographed in *W.A.I.*, i. 48.

No. 10 $\frac{48}{2}$ 31 „ „ *W.A.I.*, i. 45, 47.

Broken Cylinder, No. 11 $\frac{48}{315}$ 4, lithographed in *W.A.I.*, iii. 15, 16.

Black Stone „ *W.A.I.*, i. 49.

Broken Cylinder (unnumbered).

K 3082, K 3086, S 2027 } Containing the account of the expedition to Egypt.

K 1679. Containing the equivalent parts of lines for *W.A.I.*, i., xlv. 41, 48.

K 2671. War against Elam.

K 3053. Titles and genealogy of Esarhaddon.

K 4473. War against Sidon.

K 4444. War against Bālu, king of Tyre.

K 2663. Bears the name of Esarhaddon, dated 27th day of Iyyar.

RM. 3. Belongs to a Cylinder of Assur-bani-pal, and contains a list of names of tributary kings and cities, by which the spelling of many names in *W.A.I.*, iii. 13, has been corrected.

W.A.I., iii., xvi. No. 3. The Will of Sennacherib.

The system of transliteration adopted in the following pages is the same as that used in Professor Sayce's *Assyrian Grammar*, and is as follows :—

a - â ha	=	א
b	=	ב
g	=	ג
d	=	ד
h	=	ה
u, v	=	ו
z	=	ז
kh	=	ח
dh	=	ט
i	=	י
c	=	כ
l	=	ל
m, *also* v	=	מ
n	=	נ
's	=	ס
e	=	ע
p	=	פ
ts	=	צ
k	=	ק
r	=	ר
s	=	ש
t	=	ת

CUNEIFORM INSCRIPTIONS RELATING TO THE HISTORY OF ESARHADDON.

LIST OF EPONYMS,

B.C. 681-668.

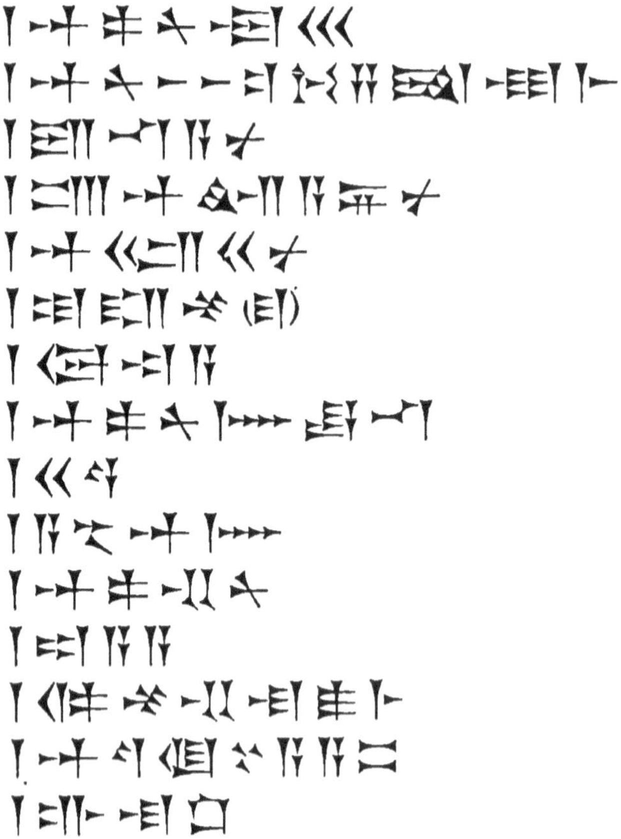

LIST OF EPONYMS

FOR EACH YEAR DURING THE REIGN OF ESARHADDON.

The Assyrian word *lim-mu* is translated "eponym" by the general consent of scholars. A *limmu*, or eponym, was appointed every year, held office for a year, and gave his name to the year. About thirty of the king's ministers had the right of being eponyms.[1]

	NAME OF EPONYM.	REFERENCE TO TABLETS.
B.C. 681,	D.P., Nabu-akhi-ures	K 288.
	D.P., Assur-akha-iddina ina D.P., cuśśu ittusib	(Canon).
	Esarhaddon upon the throne sat.	
,, 680,	D.P., Da-na-a-nu	(Canon).[2]
,, 679,	D.P., Istu-Rammanu-aninu	K 341.
,, 678,	D.P., Nergal-sar-utsur	K 1617.
,, 677,	D.P., Abu-ra-mu	(Canon).
,, 676,	D.P., Bam-ba-a	K 350.
,, 675,	D.P., Nabu-Akhi-iddina	K 1575.
,, 674,	D.P., Sar-nuri	K 285.
,, 673,	D.P., A-khaz-el	K 376.
,, 672,	D.P., Nabu-bel-utsur	K 284.
,, 671,	D.P., Dhebet-ai	K 399.
,, 670,	D.P., Sallim-bella-assib	K 327.
,, 669,	D.P., Samas-casad-aibi	K 363.
,, 668,	D.P., Mar-la-rim	K 321.

1 Eponym Canon, p. 24.

2 Mr. Smith refers to tablet K 3789 for the name of this Eponym Dananu, but the tablet is not dated, and the line of which he makes Danānu reads *inayume cas'pu iddinu*, "on the day when money they gave." (For text, see opposite page.)

W.A.I., iii. 16. No. 3.

OBVERSE.

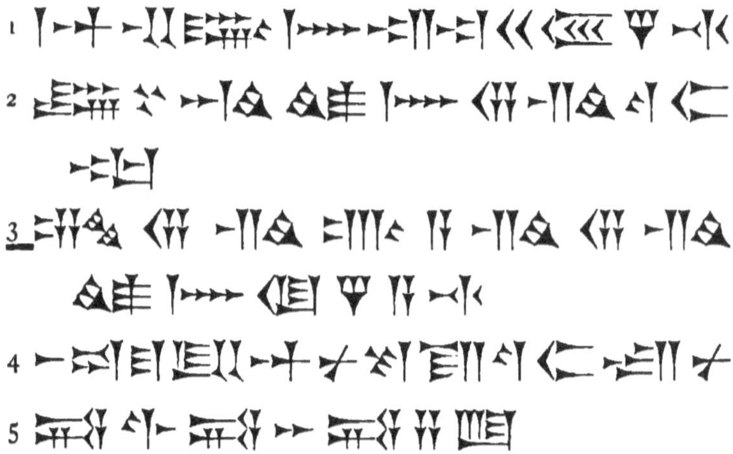

REVERSE.

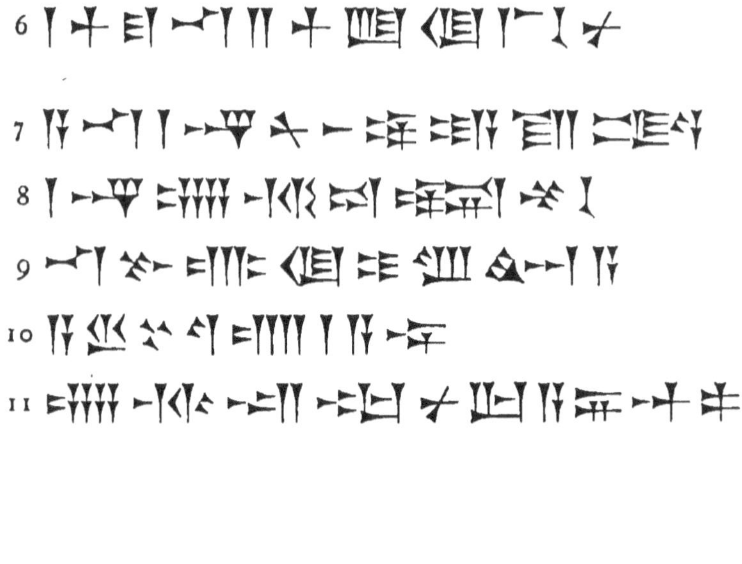

THE WILL OF SENNACHERIB.

OBVERSE.

1 D.P., D.P., Sin-akhi-irba sar cis'sati.
(I) Sennacherib, King of multitudes,
2 Sar mat Assur esiri khuratsi tulat KARNI
King of Assyria, bracelets of gold, heaps of ivory,

3 . . . . . khuratsi gāgi khuratsi esiri itti sa-a-ti (?)
a cup (?) of gold, crowns of gold, (and) chains with them,

4 ina du-ma-ki an-nu-te sa tu-lat-s'u-nu
these benefits (goods) of which there are heaps
5 D.P., ibba D.P., likh-khal D.P., zadhu
crystal stone, ... stone, bird stone.

REVERSE.

6 I bar ma-na 2 + ½ cibi ci sakal-su-nu
One and a-half manch, two and a half shekels, according to their weight
7 a-na D.P., Assur-akha-iddina abil-ya sa arcatu
to Esarhaddon my son who afterwards
8 D.P. Assur-ebil-mucin-pal sum-su
Assur-ebil-mucin-pal his name
9 na-bu-u ci-i ru-ah-a
was named according to my wish.
10 a-din cisat-tu Bit D.P., A-muk
I gave the treasure of the temple of Amuk
11 erik-irba ca-nu-ur-a-ni D.P. Nabu
irik irba the *harpists* (?) of the god Nebo.

W.A.I., i. 48. No. 2.

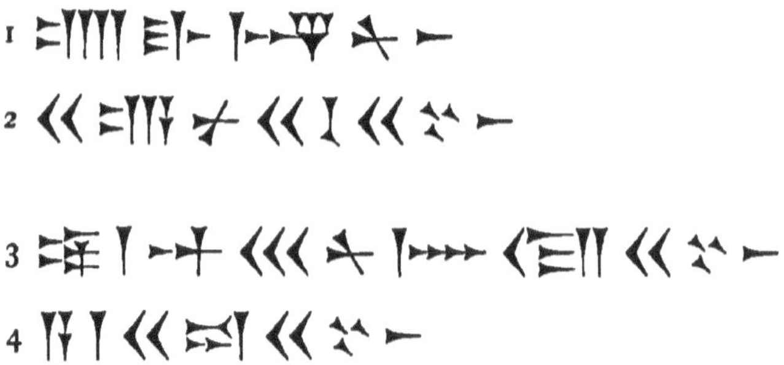

W.A.I., i. 48. No. 4.

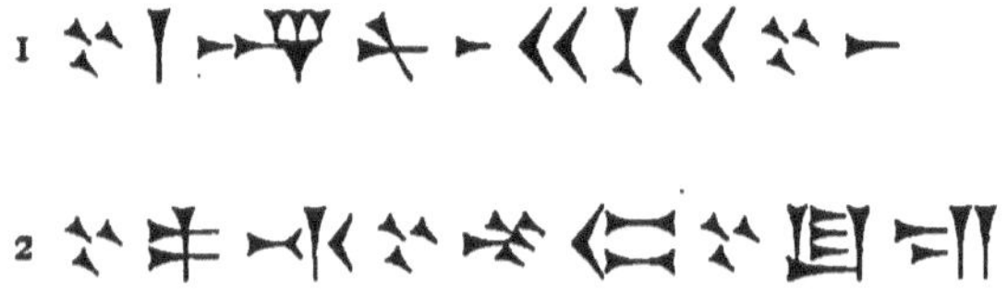

W.A.I., i. 48. No. 5.

TITLES OF ESARHADDON.

No. 2. *W.A.I.*, i. 48.

1 E-GAL D.P., Assur-akha-iddina
The palace of Esarhaddon
2 sarru dan-nu sar cis's'ati sar mat Assur
the powerful king, king of multitudes, king of the country of Assyria,
3 abil D.P., Sin-akhi-irba sar mat Assur
son of Sennacherib, king of the country of Assyria,
4 abil D.P., Sar-gin sar mat Assur
son of Sargon, king of Assyria.

No. 4. *W.A.I.*, i. 48.

1 mat D.P., Assur-akha-iddina sar ciśśati sar mat Assur
the country of Esarhaddon, king of multitudes, king of Assyria,
2 mat Khat-ti mat Mu-tsur mat Cuśi
(king of) the land of the Hittites, of Egypt, (and) Cush, (Ethiopia.)

No. 5. *W.A.I.*, i. 48.

1 a-na-cu D.P., Assur-akha-iddina-sarru rabu
I am Esarhaddon, the great king.
2 sarru dan-nu sar cis's'ati sar mat Assur sakkanak
the strong king, king of multitudes, king of Assyria, priest
3 CA-DIMIR-(RA) D.A., sar mat Sumir-D.A.
of Babylon, king of Sumir
4 u Accad D.A., sar sarri mat Mu-tsur
and Accad, king of the kings of Egypt
5 mat Khat-tu . . . . . mat Cu-s'i
of the country of the Hittites, Egypt (?) of Cush.

6 [cuneiform]
7 [cuneiform]
8 [cuneiform]
9 [cuneiform]
10 [cuneiform]

W.A.I., i. 48. No. 7.

1 [cuneiform]

W.A.I., i. 50, 1–6.

1 [cuneiform]
2 [cuneiform]
3 [cuneiform]
4 [cuneiform]
5 [cuneiform]
6 [cuneiform]

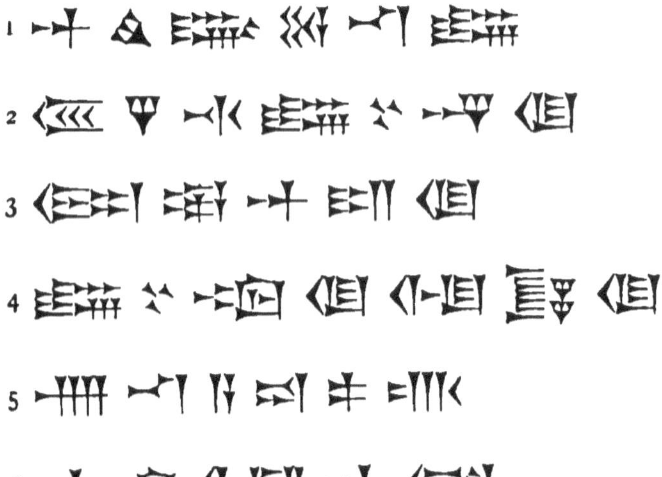

6 mat sa ci-rib D.P., Tar-bi-tsi.
(Upon) the land which is within Tarbitsi (a palace)

7 a-na mu-sab D.P., Assur-bani-pal (abla)
for the seat of Assurbanipal,

8 abil-sari rabi sa Bit-rid-u-ti
the son of the great king of the harems,

9 abil tsi-it lib-bi-ya
the son, the offspring of my body,

10 artsip u-sac-lil.
I built, I caused to be completed.

No. 7. *W.A.I.*, i. 48.

sar mat Kar-D.P. Duni-ya-as
king of the country of Kar-duniyas.

W.A.I., i. 50, 1–6.

1 D.P., Assur-akha-iddina sar
Esarhaddon king

2 ciššati sar mat Assur D.A.,
of multitudes, king of Assyria,

3 sakkanak CA-DIMIR-RA, D.A.
priest of Babylon

4 sar mat Sumir D.A., va Accad. D.A.
king of the country of Sumir and Accad,

5 rubu nā-a-du, pa-likh
the exalted prince, the worshipper of

6 D.P., Nabu va D.P., Marduk
Nebo, and Marduk.

W.A.I., iii. 15; col. 1.

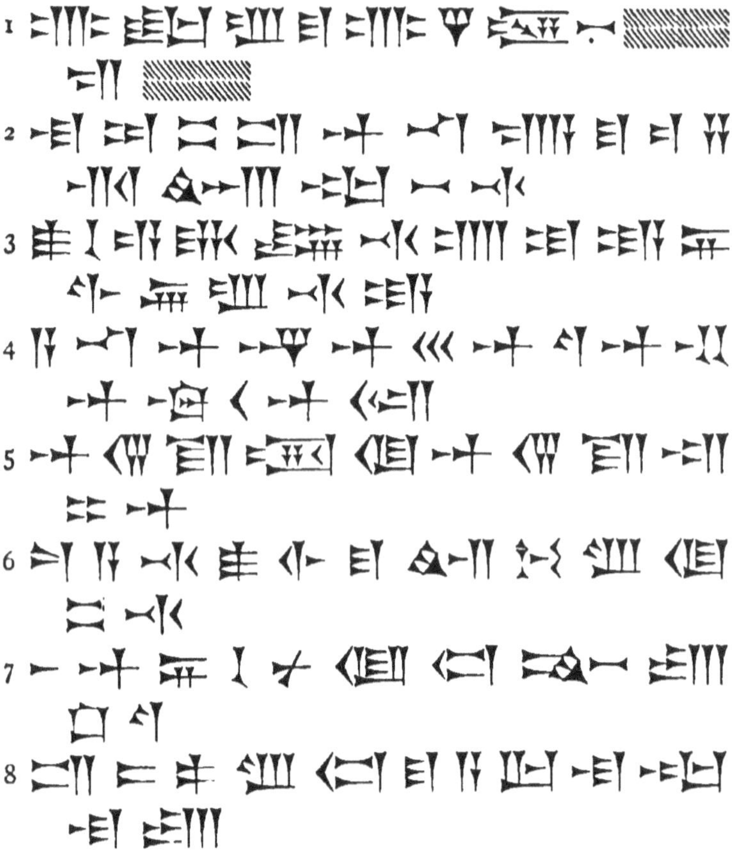

BATTLE OF ESARHADDON AGAINST HIS BROTHER, AT KHANIRABBAT, B.C. 680.

W.A.I., iii. 15; col. I.

1 u-śar-rid-va u-sa-ats-bat . . . . .
I caused to descend and I caused to take . . . . .

2 la-ab-bi-is an-na-dir-va its-tsa-ri-ikh ca-bat-ti
In heart I was discouraged, and was stricken down my liver.

3 as-su e-pis sarru-ti BIT-ABI-ya ni-pi-śa rit-ti-ya
As regards the making of the royalty of the house of my father, the extension of my dominion,

4 a-na D.P., ASSUR D.P., SIN D.P., SAMAS D.P., BEL D.P., NABU u D.P., NERGAL
to the gods Assur, Sin, Samas, Bel, Nebo, and Nergal,

5 D.P., ISTAR sa NINUA D.A., D.P., ISTAR sa D.P., ARBA-il
the goddess Istar of Nineveh, (and) the goddess Istar of Arbela,

6 Ka-a-ti as-si-va im-gu-ru ci-bi-ti
my hands I lifted up and they were kind to my prayers.

7 ina an-ni-su-nu ci-nuv SERU ta-gil-tu
By their grace established, a trusting heart (body)

8 is-tap-pa-ru-niv-va (h) a-lic la-ca-la-ta
they sent, and (said) march! do not restrain thyself

9 

10 

11 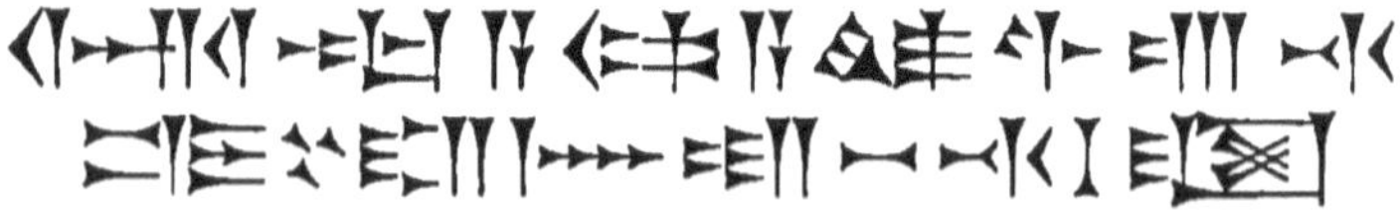

12 

13 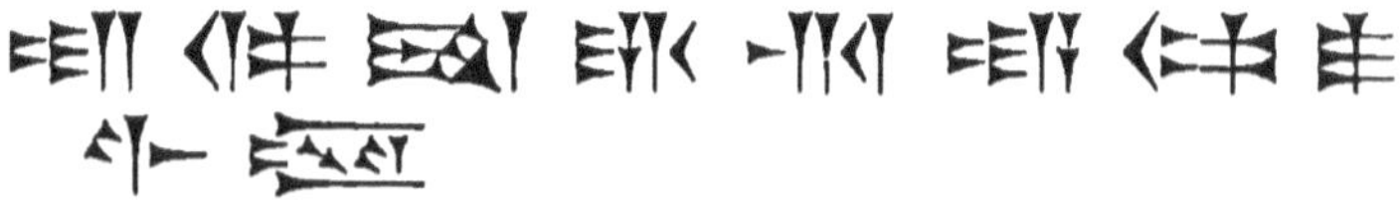

14 

15 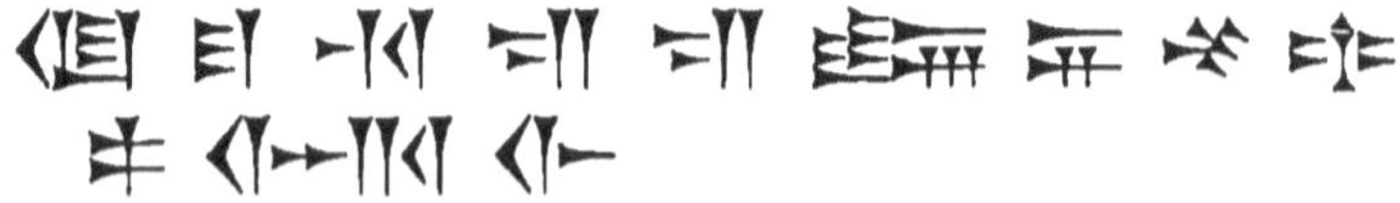

16 

17 

18 

9 i-da-a-ca- ni-it-tal-lac-va ni-na-a-ra gir-ri-a-ca
(with) thy hands, we march; and we abhor thy enemies.

10 EST-en YU-me SANNA YU-me ul uc-ci pa-an UMMANI-ya ul-at-gul
On the first day (and) second day I fought not, the front of my army I set not in array,

11 ar-ca-a ul-a-cin pi-kit-ti śUśI tsi-mit-ti NIRI
the hinder part I formed not, the overseers of the horses trained to (bear) the yoke,

12 ul u-nu-ut TAKHATSI-ya ul a-su-sur
without the furniture of my battle, I did not set in line (?)

13 tsi-di-it gir-ri-ya ul-as-pu-uc
provisions for my journey I issued not.

14 sal-gu cu-uts-tsu ARAKH SEBATTU dan-na-at en-te-na
Snow, storming (in) the month Sebat (came the) mighty darkness,
ul-a-dur
I feared not,

15 ci-ma ITSTSURI śi-śi-in-ni mu-up-pa-ar-si
like a *sisinni* bird flying

16 a-na D.P., Gab-kha-akh i-ri-tsi ap-ta-a i-da-ai
against the officer Gab-khākh, of the land (?) I opened (out) my forces;

17 Khar-ra-an NINUA D.A., pa-as-ki-is ur-ru-ukh-is ar-di-va
the road (to) Nineveh, with difficulty quickly I descended, and

18 el-la-mu-uh-a ina IRTSI-tiv mat Kha-ni-rab-bat gi-mir ku-ra-di-su-im
beyond me, in the region of the country of Khanirabbat, the whole of their warriors,

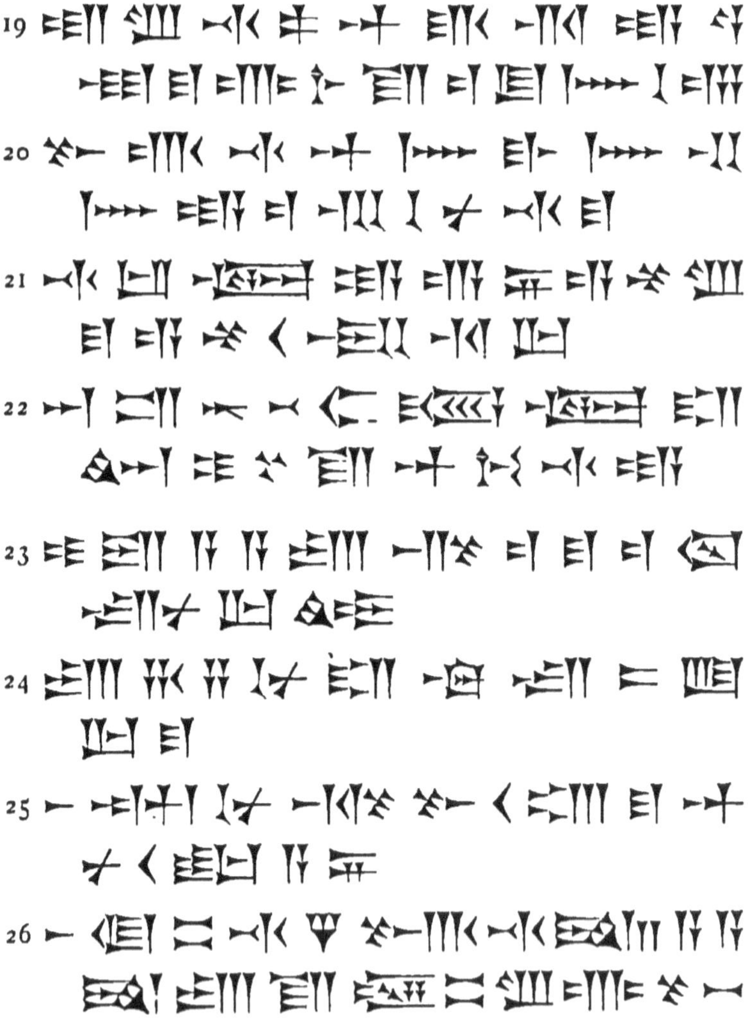

19 tsi-ru-ti pa-an gir-ri-ya tsab-tu-va u-rac-sa D.P., CACCI-su-un
powerful in front of my army placed themselves and girded on their weapons.

20 pu-lukh-ti ILI RABI BELI-ya iś-khup-su-nu-ti-va
The fear of the great gods, my lords, overwhelmed them, and

21 ti-ib TAKHATSI-ya dan-ni e-mu-v-ru-va e-mu-u makh-khu-ur
the onset of my powerful attack they saw, and collected in front.

22 D.P., Is-tar bi-lat KABALI TAKHATSI ra-ah-i-mat sa-an-gu-ti-ya
The goddess Istar, the lady of war (and) battle, the lover of my obedience,

23 i-da-ai ta-zi-iz-va D.P., MITPANI-su-nu tas-bir
my forces she fixed, their bows she broke,

24 ta-khu-tsa-su-nu ra-ac-śu tap-dhu-ur-va
their assembled fighting men she struck and

25 ina PUKHRU-su-nu nam-bu-u um-ma-an-nu yu-śar-a-ni
in their assembly disturbed, the army turns away from me.

26 ina ci-bi-ti-sa tsir-ti id-ai it-ta sa ats-bi-ru u-se-mid
By her supreme command, my hands the standard which I had raised, I caused to carry.

Broken Cylinder. *W.A.I.*, iii. 15 ; col. 2.

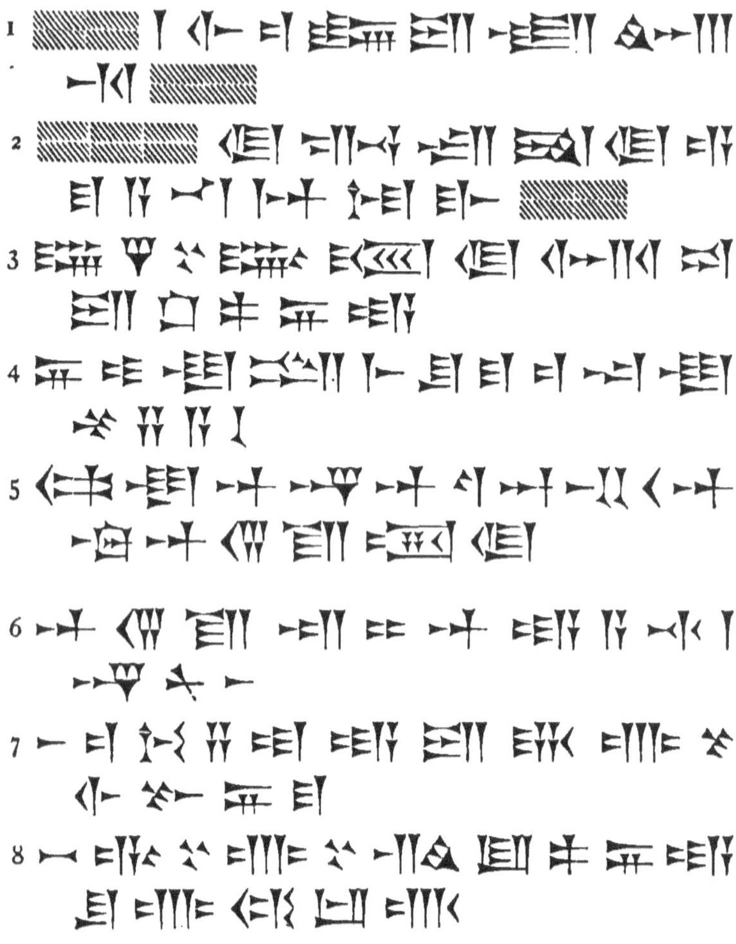

THE WAR AGAINST NABU-ZIR-NAPISTI-ESIR, SON OF MERODACH-BALADAN,

ABOUT B.C. 680.

Broken Cylinder. *W.A.I.*, iii. 15 ; col. 2.

1 . . . . in-da-li-ikh-khu . . . .
. . . . he had been troublesome . . .

2 . . . . CARASI-śu id-ci-e-va a-na D.P. NIN-GAL . . . . . .
His camp he assembled and against Nin-gal (idinna)

3 D.P. sa-nat UR-D.A. ar-du da-gil pa-ni-ya
the governor of the city Ur, a servant, a dependant upon me,

4 ni-i-tu il-ve-su-va its-ba-tu mu-tsa-a-su
battle he brought against him, and had captured his (place) of exit.

5 ul-tu D.P., AS-SUR D.P., SAMAS D.P., BEL u D.P., NABO D.P., ISTAR sa NINUA, D.A.
From (the time when) Assur, Samas, Bel and Nebo, Istar of Nineveh,

6 D.P., ISTAR sa D.P., ARBA-il ya-a-ti D.P., ASSUR-AKHA-IDINNA
Istar of Arbela, myself (namely) Esarhaddon

7 ina D.P., GU-ZA AB i-ya dha-bis u-se-si-bu-ni-va
upon the throne of my father well caused me to be seated, and

8 be-lut MATI u-sat-gi-ḷu pa-ni-ya su-u ul ip-lukh
the government of the country they caused to be entrusted to me, he himself did not reverence

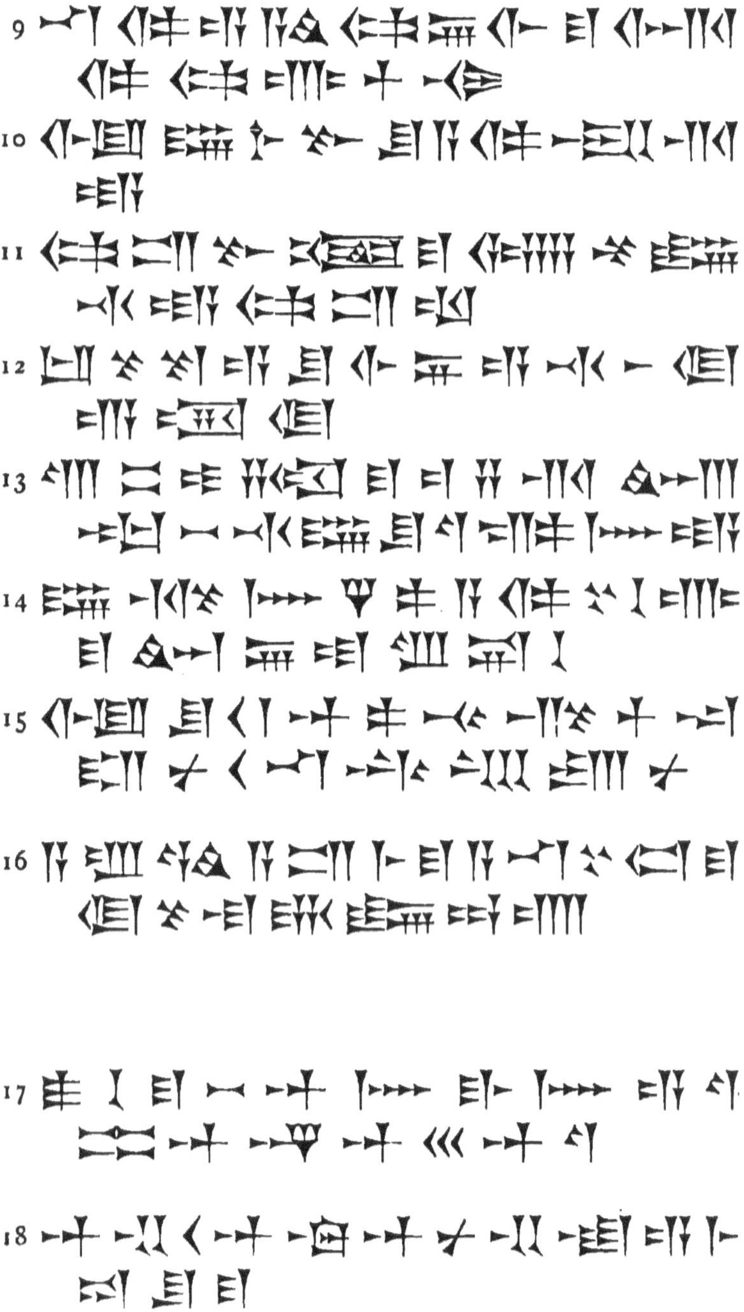

9 na-di-e a-khi ul-ir-si-va ar-di ul yu-maś-śir
the gifts of a brother he presented not, and (to do) homage he approached not,

10 va D.P., rac-bu-su a-di makh-ri-ya
and his ambassador to my presence

11 ul is-pu-rav-va sul-mu SARRU-ti-ya ul is-al
he sent not, and (concerning) the peace of my kingdom he asked not,

12 ip-se-te-e-su lim-ni-e-ti ina ci-rib NINUA. D.P., as-me-e-va
his evil deeds within Nineveh I heard, and

13 lib-bi i-gug-va its-tsa-ri-ikh ca-bat-ti D.P., su-par SAKI-ya
my heart groaned and was stricken down my liver. My officers,

14 D.P., PIKHATI sa pa-a-di MATI-su u-ma-ah-ir tsi-ru-us-su
the prefects of the borders of his country I hastened against him,

15 va-su-u D.P., NABU-ZIR-NAPISTI-ESIR ba-ra-nu u
and he (namely) Nabu-zir-napisti-esir, gross (?) and
na-pal-cat-ta-nu
a rebel,

16 a-lac UMMANI-ya is-me-va a-na mat Ela-ma, D.A., se-la-pis
of the march of my army heard, and to the country of Elam, like a fox
in-na-bit.
he fled away.

17 as-su ma-mit ILI RABI e-par-ku, D.P., AS-SUR, D.P., SIN, D.P., SAMAS
Since the covenant of the great gods he had broken, Assur, Sin, Samas,

18 D.P., BEL u D.P., NABU au-nu en-tu e-me-du-su-va
Bel and Nebo, sin (and) guilt placed upon him,

19 

20 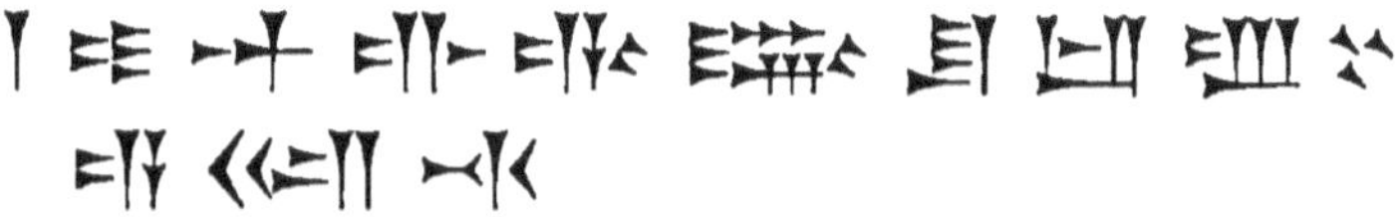

21 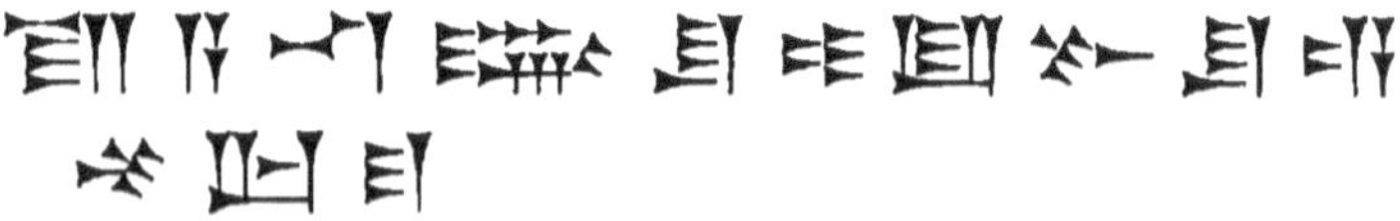

22 

23 

24 

25 

26 

19 ci-rib MAT Ela-ma D.A., i-na-ru-su ina cacc(i)
within the land of Elam they overwhelmed him with weapons.

20 D.P., NAHID D.P., Mar-duk AKH-su ip-sit MAT E-lam-ti
Nahid-Merodach his brother, of the matter (in) the country of Elam,

21 sa a-na AKH-su i-tib-bu-su e-mu-ur-va
which to his brother had happened, saw and

22 ul-tu MAT E-lam-ti in-nab-tu-va a-na e-pis ARD-u-ti-ya
from the country of Elam had fled and to make submission to me, (lit. "my homage.")

23 a-na MAT ASSUR D.A., il-lic-av-va yu-tsal-la-a bi-lu-ti
to the country of Assyria came and he besought (prayed) my lordship.

24 MAT tam-tiv a-na śi-khir-ti-sa ri-du-ut AKHI-su u-sat-gil
The sea coast, to its whole extent, the dominion of his brother, I
pa-nu-us-su
entrusted to him.

25 sat-ti sam-ma la-na-par-ca-a it-ti ta-mar-ti-su ca-bit-te
Yearly a sum unvarying with his numerous presents

26 a-na NINUA D.A., i-lic-av-va yu-na-as-sa-ka SEPA-ya
to Nineveh he came and he kissed my two feet.

EXPEDITION AGAINST ABDI-MILCUTTI KING OF SIDON, AND SĀNDUARRI, KING OF CUNDI AND S'IZŪ.

W.A.I., i. 45 ; col. 1.

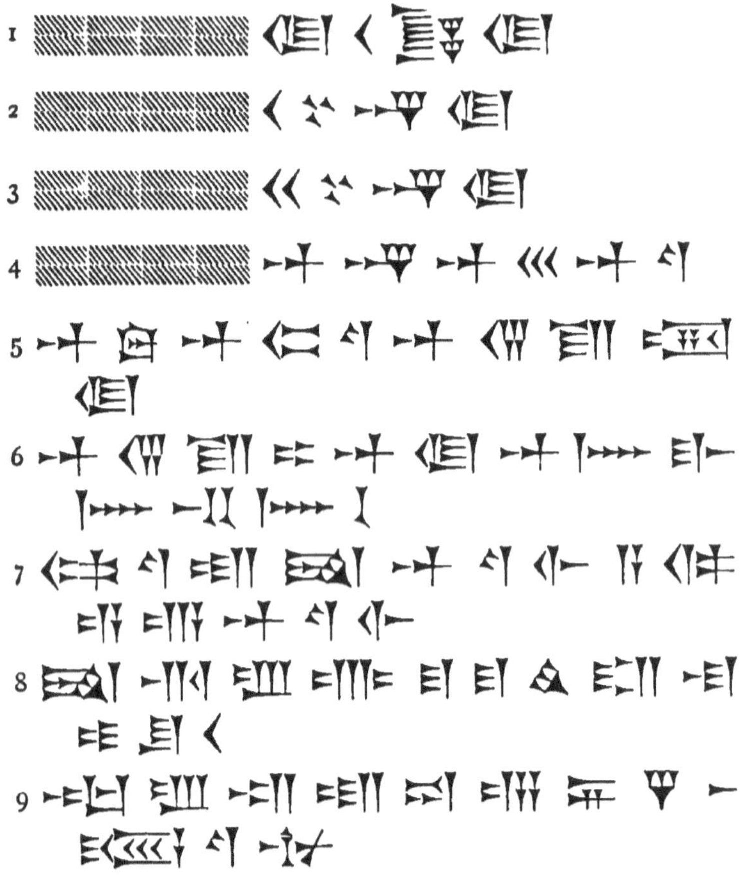

EXPEDITION AGAINST ABDI-MILCUTTI, KING OF SIDON, AND SĀNDUARRI, KING OF CUNDI AND S'IZŪ.

W.A.I., i. 45 ; col. I.

British Museum, Number 10—31 (48 above, 2 below)

1 . . . . D.A., u Accad D.A.
. . . . (Sumir) and Accad

2 . . . . u MAT ASSUR, D.A.
. . . . and the country of Assyria

3 . . . . sar mat Assur, D.A.
. . . . king of the country of Assyria,

4 . . . . D.P. ASSUR P.P., SIN D.P. SAMAS,
. . . . the gods Assur, Sin, Samas,

5 D.P. NABU D.P., MARDUK D.P., ISTAR sa NINUA, D.A.
Nebo, Marduk, the goddess Istar of Nineveh,

6 D.P., ISTAR sa ARBA-il D.A. ILI RABI BELI-su
the goddess Istar of Arbela, the great gods his lords,

7 ul-tu tsi-it D.P., Sam-si a-di e-rib D.P., Sam-si
(who) from the rising of the sun to the setting of the sun

8 it-tal-lac-u-va ma-khi-ra la-i-su-u
he hath marched, and an opponent has not had.

9 Ca-sid D.P., Tsi-du-un-ni sa ina GABAL tam-tiv
The conqueror of Tsidon, which (is) upon the border of the sea,

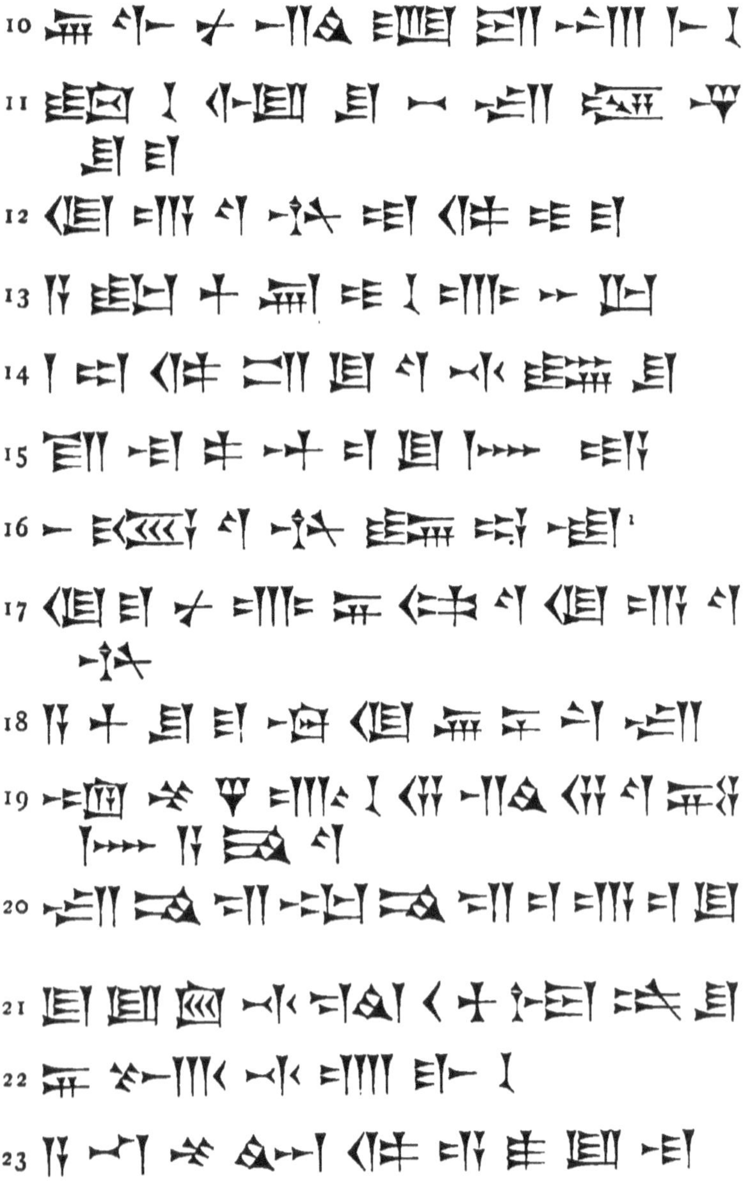

[1] Compare

10 śa-pi-nu gi-mir da-ad-me-su
sweeping away all its inhabitants,

11 DUR-su va su-bat-śu aś-śur-su-va
its fortress, and its site I captured and

12 ci-rib tam-tiv ad-di-i-va
into the midst of the sea I cast and

13 a-sar mas-gan-i-su u-khal-lik
the region of its habitation I desolated.

14 D.P., Ab-di-mil-cu-ut-ti SAR-su
Abdi-milcūtti its king

15 sa la-pa-an D.P., CACCI-ya
who from before my weapons

16 ina KABAL tam-tiv in-nab-tu
into the midst of the sea had fled[1]

17 ci-ma nu-u-ni ul-tu ci-rib-tam-tiv
like a fish, from the midst of the sea

18 a-mas-su-va ac-ci śa kak-ka-śu
I drew him out and cut off his head.

19 nac-mu NAMCUR-SU KHURATSU CAŚPU ABNI a-kar-tav
Spoiling his goods, gold, silver, precious stones,

20 MAŚAC RIMI KARAN RIMI D.P., DAN D.P., SUBTU
skin of the wild bull, horn of the wild bull, strong wood, chair wood,

21 D.P., lu-bul-ti BIRMI u CITU NIN-SUM-SU
clothing, variegated and linen, whatever its name

22 ni-tsir-ti E-GAL-su
the treasures of his palace,

23 a-na mu-ah-di-e as-lu-la
to a great (number) I carried off

[1] Compare ci-ma NUNI its-bat su-pul MIE ru-ku-ti
like the fishes he took (went into) the depth of distant waters.

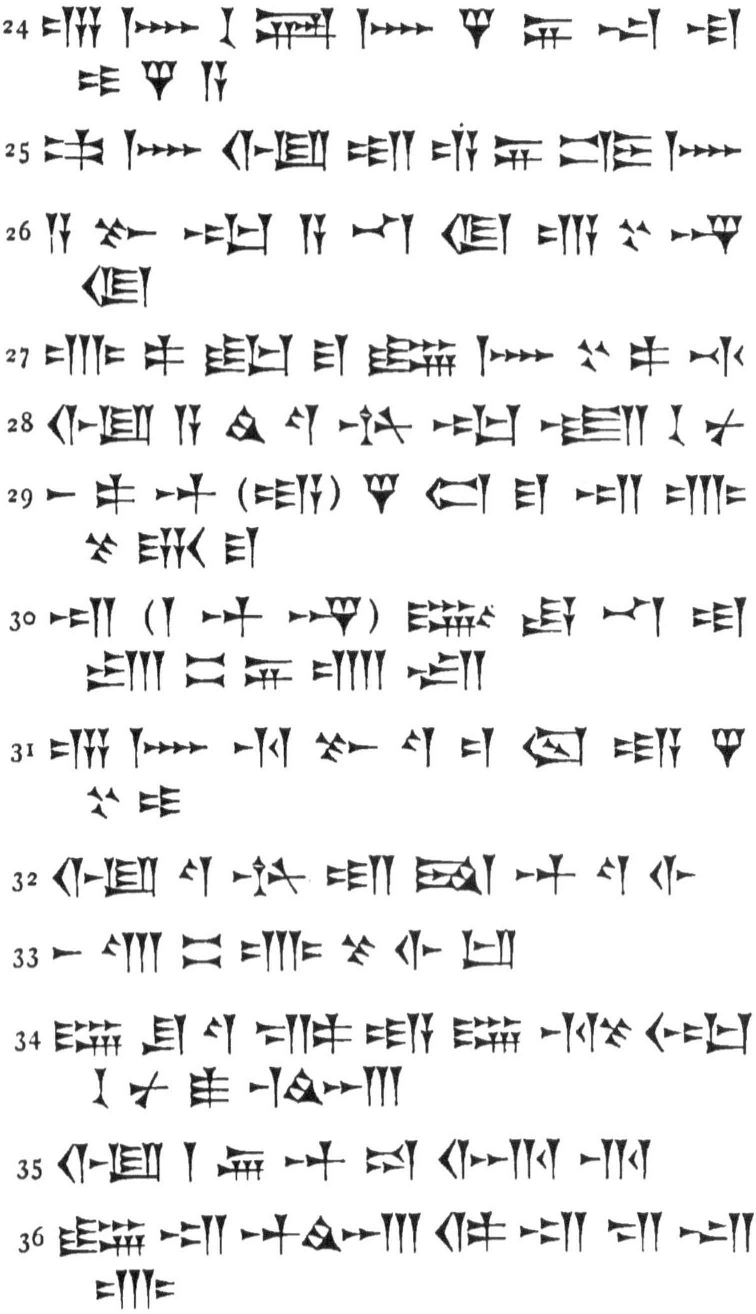

24 NISI-su UMMI sa ni-ba la i-sa-a
His men (and) women which number had not

25 ALPI va tsi-e-ni IMIRI
oxen and sheep, asses

26 a-bu-ca a-na ci-rib MAT ASSUR D.A.,
I turned (drove) to the midst of the country of Assyria.

27 u-pa-khir-va SARRANI MAT khat-ti
I assembled also the kings of the land of the Hittites,
28 va a-khi tam-tiv ca-li-su-nu
and the sea coast the whole of them
29 ina pa-an-(ya) sa nuv-va ALU u-se-pis-va
into my presence. Another city I caused to make and

30 AL (D.P., D.P., ASSUR) AKHA-IDDIN-na at-ta-bi ni-bit-śu
the city of Esarhaddon, I called its name

31 NISI khu-bu-ut D.P., MITPANI-ya sa SAD-i
the men, the spoil of my bow from the mountains.

32 va tam-tiv tsi-id D.P., Sam-si
and the sea of the rising sun
33 ina lib-bi u-se-si-ib
in the midst of (it) I caused to dwell
34 D.P., su-par-SAK ya D.P., PIKHATU eli-su-nu as-cun
my general as prefect over them I established,

35 va D.P., śa-an-du-ar-ri
and S'ānduarri
36 SAR ALI Cun-di D.P., S'i-zu-u
king of the city Cundi, (and) the city S'izū,

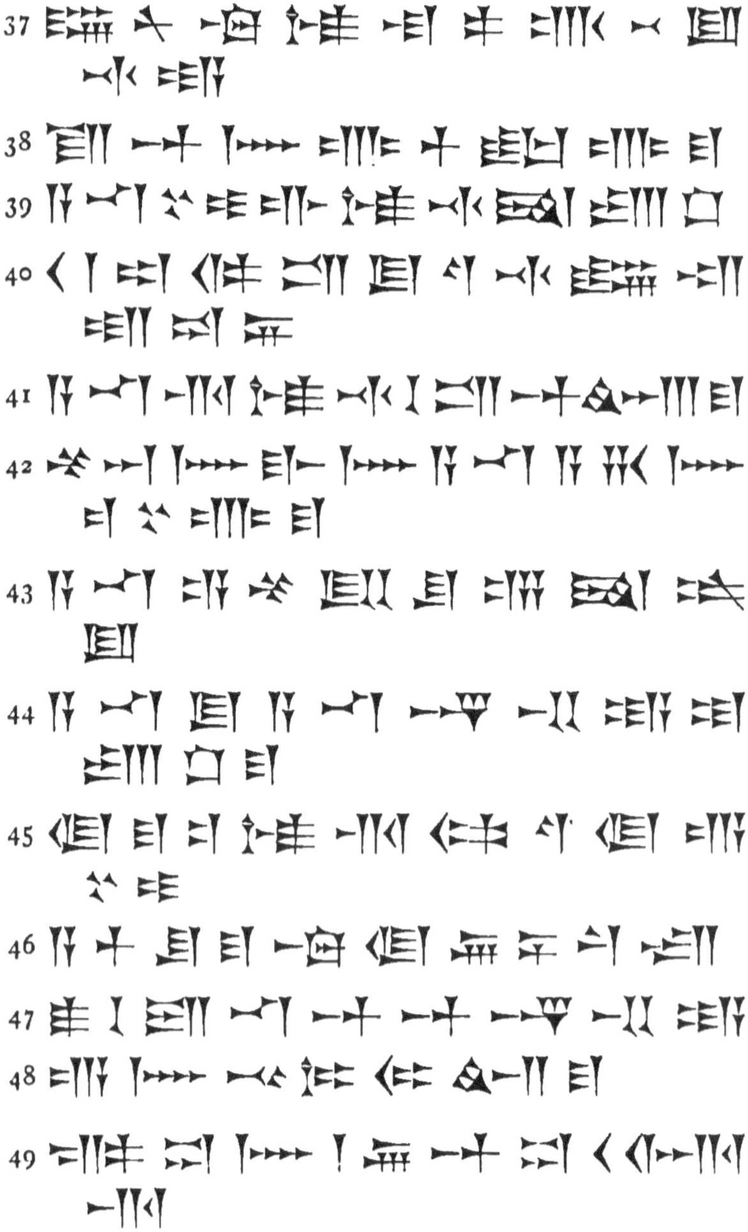

37 D.P., NACIRU ak-tsu la pa-lakh be-lu-ti-ya
an enemy, destroying, not a reverer of my lordship,

38 sa ILI yu-maś-śar-u-va
whom the gods had deserted, and

39 a-na SAD-i mar-tsu-ti it-ta-gil
to the rugged mountains trusted

40 u D.P., Ab-di-mil-cu-ut-ti SAR AL Tsi-du-ni
also Abdi-milcūtti, king of the city Tsidon

41 a-na ri-tsu-ti-su is-cun-va
to his help established (got) and

42 SUM ILI RABI a-na a-kha-i iz-cur-u-va[1]
the name of the great gods to each other they remembered, and

43 a-na e-mu-ki-su-un it-tag-lu
to their forces they trusted.

44 a-na-cu a-na ASSUR BIL-ya at-ta-gil-va
But I, to Assur my lord trusted, and

45 ci-ma its-tsu-ri ul-tu ci-rib SAD-i
like a bird from within the mountain,

46 a-mas-su-va ac-ci-śa kak-ka-śu
I drew him out and I cut off his head.

47 as-su da-na-an D.P., ASSUR BIL-ya
Besides, by the might of Assur, my lord,

48 NISI cul-luv mi-im-ma
the men all of them, whoever (they were,)

49 KAKKADI D.P., S'a-an-du-u-ar-ri
the heads of S'ānduarri

[1] Compare וּבְשֵׁם אֱלֹהֵיהֶם לֹא־תַזְכִּירוּ Joshua xxii. 7, "Neither make mention (remember) the name of their gods."

50 

51 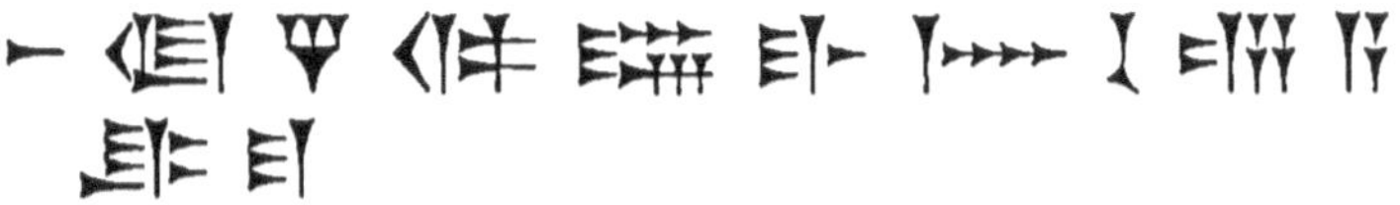

52 

53 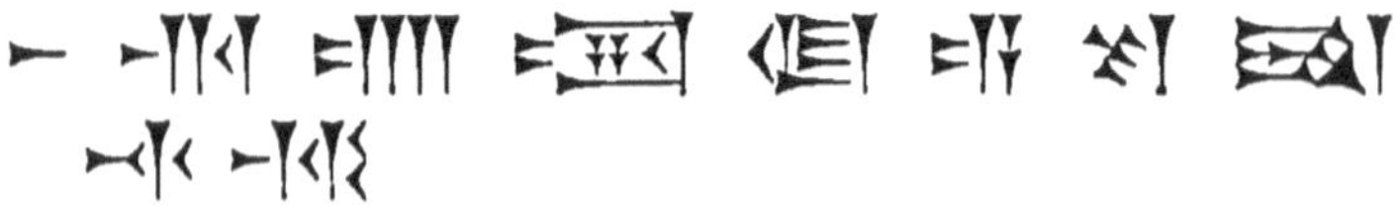

54 

55 

EXPEDITION AGAINST THE CIMMERI AND CILICIA.

W.A.I., i. 45 ; col. 2.

1 

2 

3 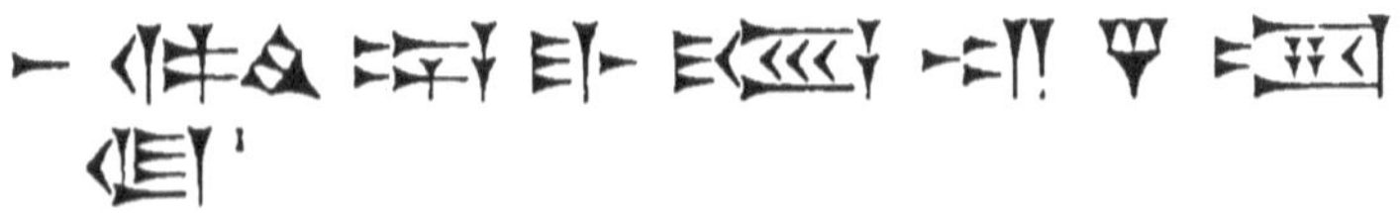 [1]

4 

[1] Compare 
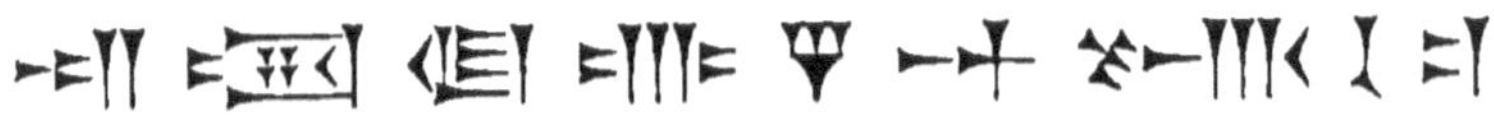
 (*W.A.I.*, iii., 25, 93).

50 va, D.P., Ab-di-mi-il-cu-ut-ti
and Abdi-milcūtti

51 ina ci-sa-di NIS(I) RABI-su-nu a-lul-va
upon the necks of their great men I hung and

52 it-ti, D.P., NINGUTI, u . . . . ZICARI U SINNISTI . . . .
together with the musicians, both male and female . . . .

53 ina ri-bit NINUA, D.A., e-te-it-ti-ik
through the wide spaces of Nineveh, I made pass through.

54 sa-lil AL Ar-za-ni
spoiler of the city Arzain,

55 .. . . na . . . . . MAT Mu-uts-ri
. . . . of the country of Egypt.

EXPEDITION AGAINST THE CIMMERI AND CILICIA.

W.A.I., i. 45; col. 2.

1 . . . . id-ci-e-su
. . . . he gathered it

2 a-na MAT AS-SUR, D.A., u-ra-a
to the country of Assyria I brought.

3 inà di-khi ABULLI GABAL AL-sa NINUA, D.A.[1]
In front of the great gate at the border of the city Nineveh,

4 it-ti A-ŚI CALBI DABI
with wild bulls, (?) dog(s and) bear(s).

[1] Compare ina BAB tsi-it, D.P., Sam-si gabal, D.P., NINUA, D.A., u-sa-an-tsir-su, D.P., si-ga-ru. In the gate of the rising sun, at the border of Nineveh, I caused him to be guarded in wooden bonds.—*W.A.I.*, iii. 25, 93.

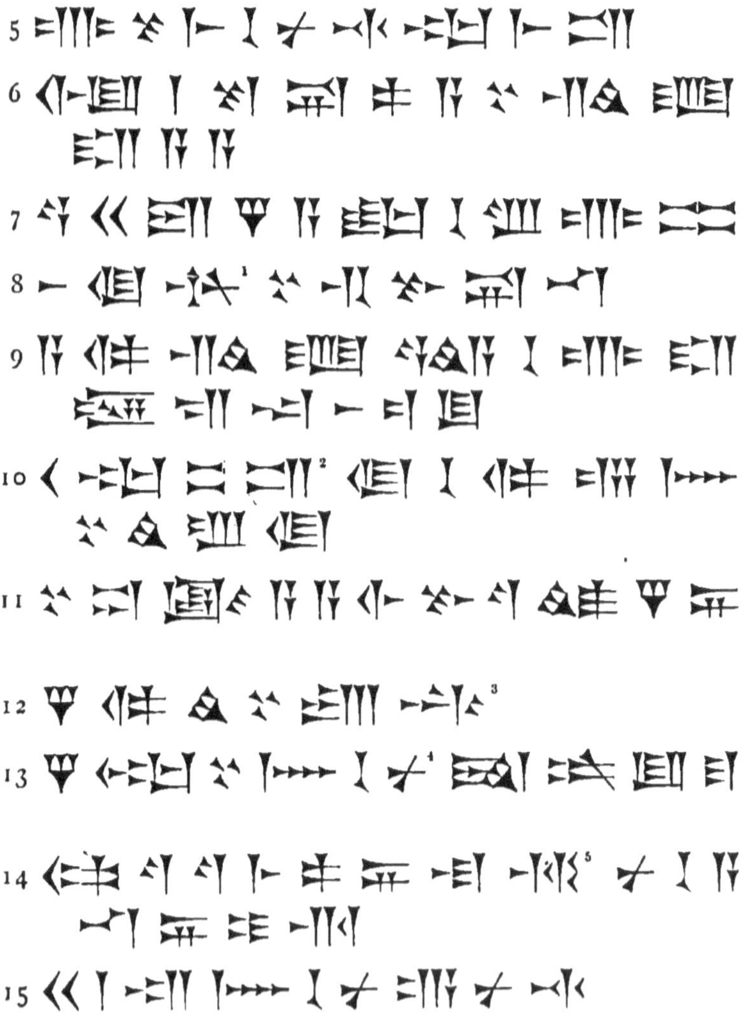

5 [cuneiform]
6 [cuneiform]
7 [cuneiform]
8 [cuneiform]
9 [cuneiform]
10 [cuneiform]
11 [cuneiform]
12 [cuneiform]
13 [cuneiform]
14 [cuneiform]
15 [cuneiform]

[1] [cuneiform] (W.A.I. iii., 15, 1).
[2] [cuneiform] (W.A.I. iii., 15, 3).
[3] [cuneiform] (W.A.I. iii., 15, 5).
[4] [cuneiform] (inserted here by W.A.I. iii., 15, 6).
[5] [cuneiform] (W.A.I. iii., 15, 6).

5 u-se-sib-su-nu-ti ca-me-is
I caused them to dwell in a heap,
6 va, D.P., Te-us-pa-a MAT Gi-mir-ra-ai
and Teuspā (king) of the country of the Gimirrai,

7 TSAB man-da sa a-sar-su ru-u-ku
a barbarous (?) soldier, whose country (is) remote (namely)
8 ina IRTSI-tiv MAT Khu-pu-us-na
in the territory of the country of Khupūsna,
9 a-di gi-mir UMMANI-su u-ra-aś-śi-ba ina CACCI
together with the whole of his army, I ran through with the sword;

10 u-ca-bi-is ci-su-di NISI MAT khi-lac-ci
(and) I trampled (upon) the necks of the men of the country of Cilicia,
11 MAT Du-uh-a a-si-bu-ut khar-sa-ni
(and) the country of Dūha, the inhabitants of the forests (*or* hills)
12 sa di-khi MAT Ta-bal
which (are) opposite the country of Tabal (*or* Ta-ba-la),
13 sa eli SADI-su-nu (dan-nu-ti) it-tag-lu-va
who upon (the strength) of their mountains (strong) had trusted, and
14 ul-tu YU-me pa-ni la ic-nu-su a-na ni-i-ri
from the days of old did not submit to my yoke,

15 XX + I ALANI-su-nu dan-nu-ti
twenty-one of their strong cities,

16 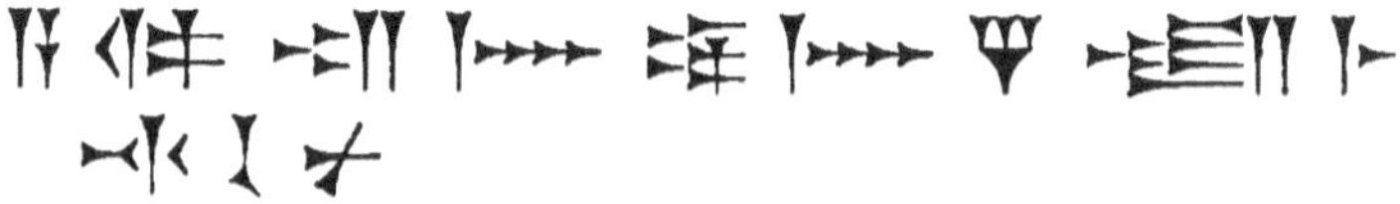

17 

18 

19 

20 

21 

22 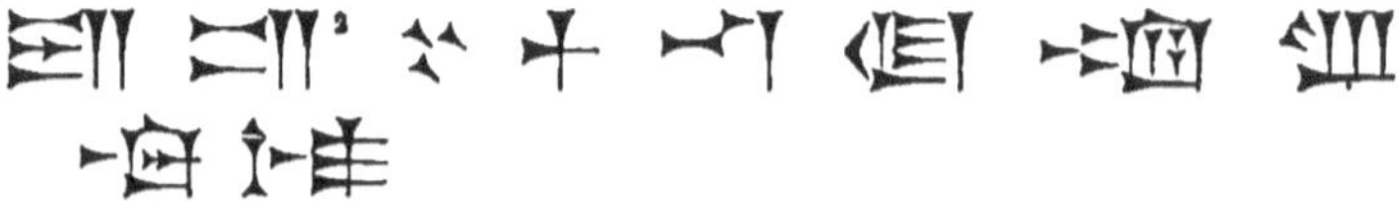

23 

24 

25 

26 

27 

28 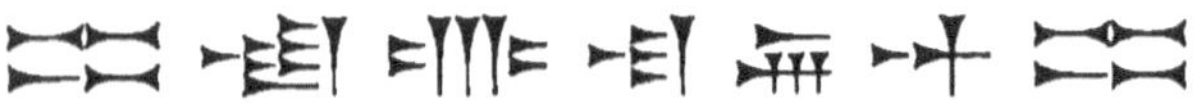

[1]  (*W.A.I.* iii., 15, 10).

[2]  (*W.A.I.* iii., 15, 13).

[3] 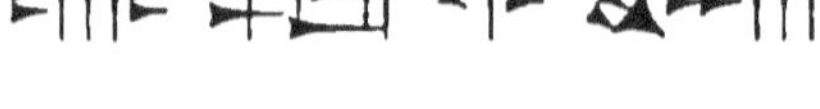 (*W.A.I.* iii., 15, 16).

16 a-di ALANI TSAKHRI sa li-ve-ti-su-nu
together with the small cities which bordered them

17 al-ve ac-sud as-lu-la sal-lat-sun
I besieged, I captured, I spoiled (them) of their spoil;
18 ab-bul ag-gur ina ISATI ac-vu
I threw down, I dug up, with fire I burned.
19 śi tu-te-su-nu sa khi-idh-dhu
The remainder of them, who rebellion
20 va kul-lul-tav la i-su-u
and curses had not (uttered),
21 cab-tu ni-ir be-lu-ti-ya e-mid-su-nu-ti
the heavy yoke of my lordship I placed (stood) upon them.

22 Da-is (*var.* ad-is) MAT Par-na-ci nac-ru ak-tsu
The trampler (I trampled upon) the country of Parnaci, an enemy, destroying
23 a-si-bu-ut MAT TUL-a-sur-ri
the inhabitants of the country of Tel-Assur,
24 sa i-na pi-i NISI
which in the language of the men (natives)
25 AL me-ekh-ra-nu D.P., Pi-ta-a-nu
of the city Mēkhranu, the city Pitānu

26 i-nam-bu-u zi-cir-su-un
they call their name.
27 mu-sap-pi-ikh (*var.* u-sap-pi-ikh) NISI MAT Man-na-ai
The scatterer of (I scattered) the men of the country of Van,
28 Ku-tu-u la śa-an-ku
Gutium disobedient,

29 

30 

31 

32 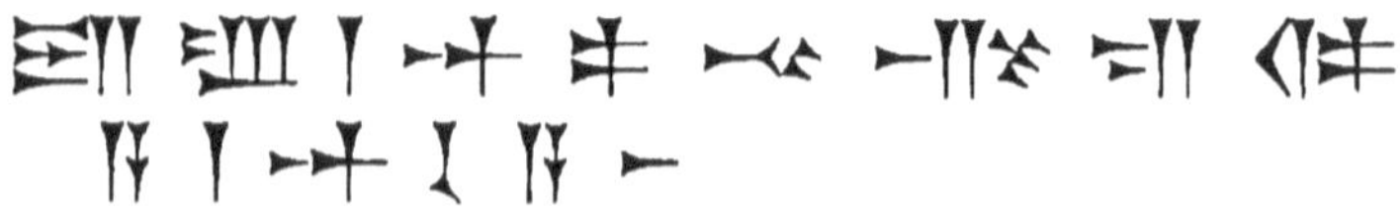

33 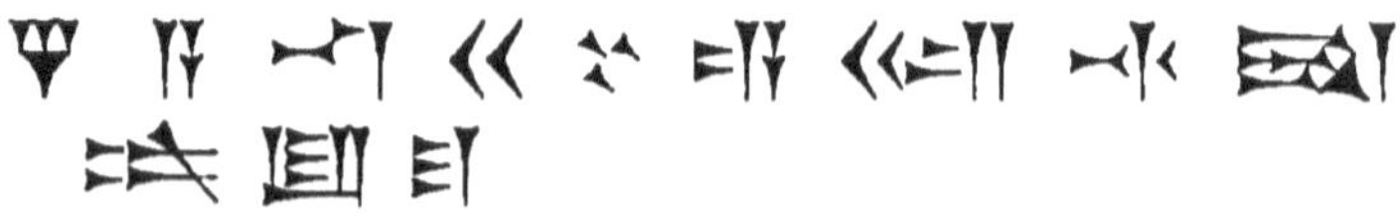

34 

35 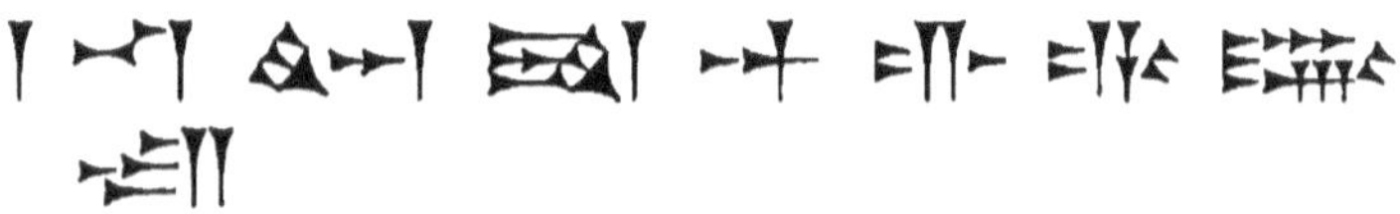

36 

37 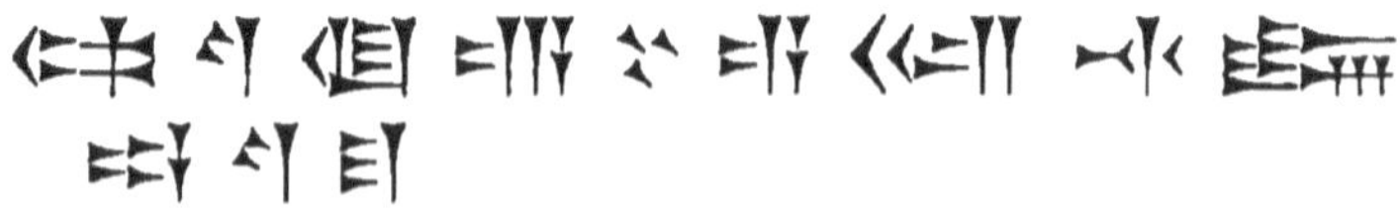

38 

39 

40 

[1]  (*W.A.I.* iii., 15, 17).

[2]  (*W.A.I.* iii., 15, 18).

29 sa um-ma-na-a-ti (*var.* UMMANU) D.P., Is-pa-ca-ai
who the armies of Ispacai (king of)

30 MAT As-gu-za-ai mā-ru la mu-se-zi-bi-su
the country of the Asguzāi, a rebel force, not saving him,

31 i-na-ru (*var.* a-na-ar) ina CACCI
had overwhelmed (I overwhelmed) with weapons.
32 Dha-rid, D.P., D.P., NABU-ZIR-NAPISTI-ESIR ABIL, D.P., D.P. MARDUK-ABLA-IDINNA
The repeller of Nabu-zir-napisti-esir, son of Merodach-Baladan,
33 sa a-na SAR MAT E-lam-ti it-tag-lu-va
who to the king of the country of Elam had trusted and

34 la u-se-zi-bu nap-sat-śu
had not caused his life to be saved.
35 D.P. Na-ah-id D.P., Mar-duk AKH-śu
Nahid-Merodach, his brother,

36 As-su e-pis ARD-u-ti-ya
in order to make my submission (*i.e.*, submission to me),
37 ul-tu ci-rib MAT E-lam-ti in-nab-tu-va
from within the country of Elam had fled, and

38 a-na NINUA D.A. AL be-lu-ti-ya
to Nineveh, the city of my lordship
39 il-lic-av-va yu-na-as-si-ik SEPĀ-ya
came and kissed my feet.

40 MAT tam-tiv a-na śi-khi-ir-ti-sa
The country of the sea (*i.e.*, sea-coast) to its whole extent,

41 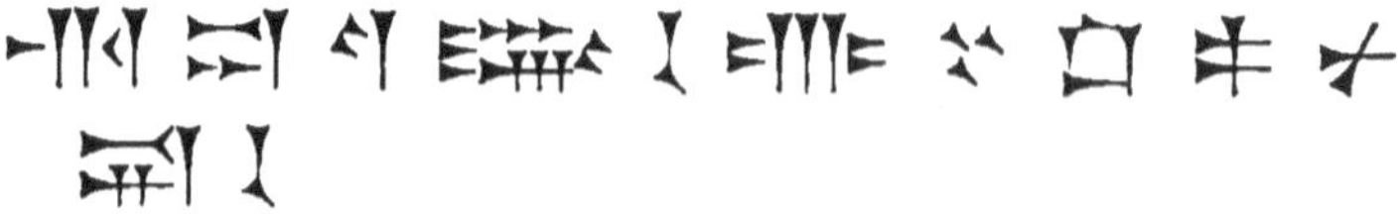

42 

43 

44 

45 

46 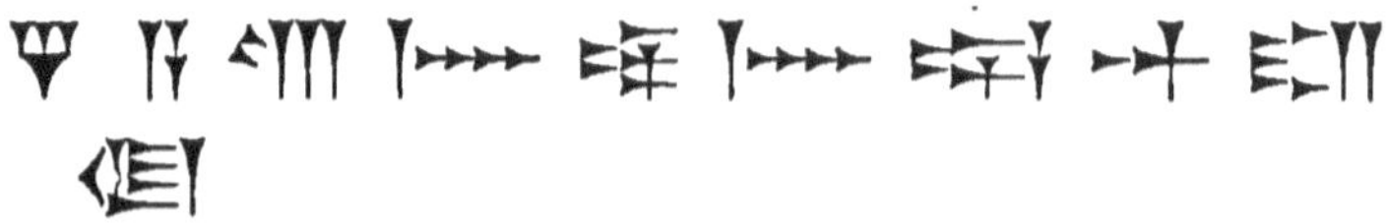

47 

48 

1  (*W.A.I.* iii. 15, 19).

2  (*W.A.I.* iii. 15, 20).

3  (*W.A.I.* iii. 15, 21).

4 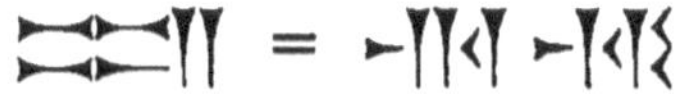 (*W.A.I.* iii., 15, 23).

5  *yu-tir-ru ra-ma-nu-us*, "they turned themselves away," is inserted after *ra* by *W.A.I.* iii., 15, 23.

41 ri-du-ut AKH-su u-sat-gil pa-nu-us-su
the dominion of his brother I caused to be entrusted to him.

42 Na-bi-ah (*var.* as-lul) MAT BIT, D.P., Dak-kur-ri
The disturber of (I spoiled) the country of Beth-Dakkurri,
43 sa ci-rib MAT Kal-di ai-ab CA-DIMIR(RA) D.A.
which (is) within the land of Chaldea, an enemy of Babylon,

44 ca-mu-u (*var.* ac-vu), D.P., D.P., SAMAS-ib-ni SAR-śu
the burner of (I burned) Samas-ibni its king
45 iś-khap-pu khab-bi-lu la pa-li-khu zic-ri BELI
a ravager wicked, not revering the memory of the lords,

46 sa EKILI ABLÎ CA DIMIR-RA, D.A.,
who the lands of the sons of Babylon (Babylonians)

47 u Bar-sap, D.A., ina pa-ri-ik-te it-ba-lu-va
and Borsippa, by violence had carried away. And

48 as-su a-na-cu pu-lukh-ti, D.P., BEL u, D.P., NABU i-du-u
as for myself, the fear of the gods Bel and Nebo I knew.

49 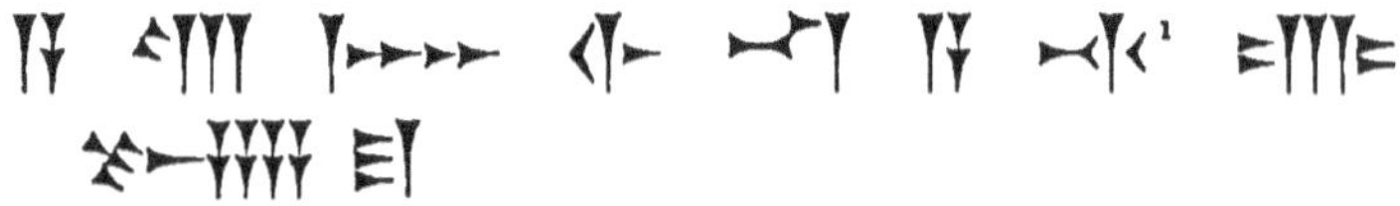

50 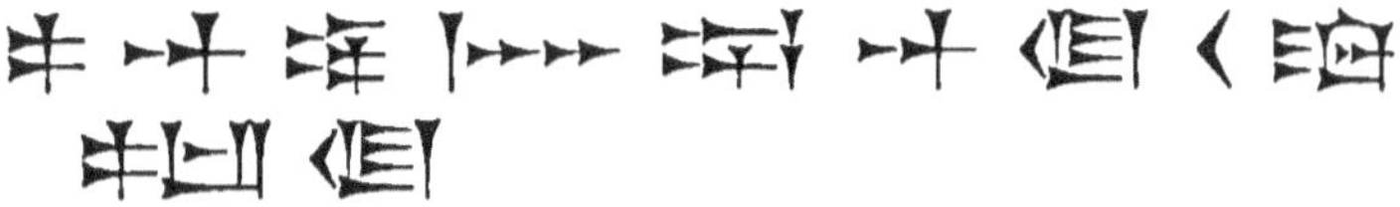

51 

52 

53 

54 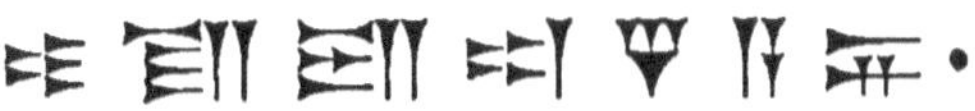

[1]  (*W.A.I.* iii. 15, 25).

49 ECILI si-na-a-ti (*var.* sa-ti-na) u-tir-va
Those lands I restored, and

50 pa-an ABLI CA DIMIR-RA, D.A., u Bar-sap, D.A.,
to the sons (inhabitants) of Babylon and Borsippa

51 u-sat-gil
I caused to be entrusted.

52 D.P., D.P., NABU-sal-lim ABIL, D.P., Ba-la-śu
Nebo-sallim, son of Balaśu,

53 ina, D.P., GU-ZA-su u-se-sib-va
upon his throne I caused to be seated, and

54 i-sa-dha ap-sa-a-nï
he repented of his transgressions (*or*, he performed acts of homage).

THE ARABIAN WAR OF ESARHADDON.

In lines 55 and 56, printed below, it is stated that Sennacherib had conquered the city of Edom, in Arabia. A notice of this event is found on a tablet (K 3405), very much defaced, a copy of which is printed in Smith's *Sennacherib*, p. 138. The invasion by Sennacherib took place about B.C. 691. At the time of Esarhaddon, Khazail was king of Arabia, and when he died Esarhaddon bestowed the throne upon Yautāh or Yāhlua, the son of Khazail. This occurred during the reign of Esarhaddon, and Yautah paid his appointed tribute, as Khazail had done before him, until some time after the death of Esarhaddon. Assur-bani-pal, was king of Assyria, and Saulmugina, his brother, had revolted. It was then that Yautah joined in the revolt and raised two armies; one he sent to Palestine, and the other to the help of the Babylonians. He had refused to pay his tribute, and his conduct is thus tersely described by Assur-bani-pal (*W.A.I.*, iii. 23, 105):—"For when Elam was speaking sedition with Accad, he heard, and then he disregarded fealty to me, (even) myself Assur-bani-pal, the King, the noble hero, the powerful chief, the work of the hands of the god Assur. He forsook me, and to Abiyateh and Aimu, sons of Teahri, his forces with them, for the assistance of Saulmugina, my rebellious brother, he sent, and established his face. The people of Arabia he caused to revolt with him, and carried off the plunder of the people whom Assur, Istar, and the great gods had given me." His was, however, totally defeated, for another notice says—"The Arabians who escaped from before my warriors the god Ninip destroyed. In want and famine their life was passed, and for food they eat the flesh of their children. . . . . To Yautah misfortune happened, and he fled away alone to Nabāiti." Assur-bani-pal placed Abiyāteh upon the throne of Yautāh." The account of these events, given in *W.A.I.*, iii. 25, 81, goes on to state that Assur-bani-pal brought Yautāh out from Nabatea, and kept him chained in the Gate of the Rising Sun, in Nineveh.

THE ARABIAN WAR OF ESARHADDON.

W.A.I., i. 45 ; col. 2, 55–58.

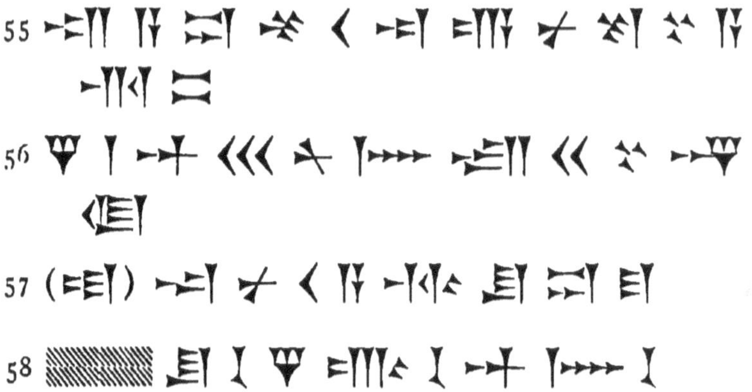

W.A.I., i. 46 ; col. 3.

THE ARABIAN WAR OF ESARHADDON.

W.A.I., i. 45; col. 2, 55–58.

55 D.P., A-du-mu-u al dan-nu-te MAT A-ri-bi
(To) the city of Edom, a fortified city of the country of Arabia

56 sa, D.P., D.P., SIN-AKHI-ARBA SAR MAT ASSUR, D.A.,
which Sennacherib, king of the land of Assyria,

57 (ABU) ba-nu-u-a ic-su-du-va
the father, my begotter, had conquered, and

58 (bus)-su-su NAMCUR-su ILI-su
its wealth, its riches, its gods.

W.A.I., i. 46; col. 3.

1 (is-lu-la) a-na MAT ASSUR, D.A.,
had carried away to the country of Assyria.

2 . . . . u-ra-a
. . . . I brought

3 D.P., Kha-za-a-il sa MAT A-ri-bi
Khazāil (king) of the land of Arabia,

4 it-ti ta-mar-ti-su ca-bit-te
with his numerous presents,

5 a-na NINUA, D.A., AL be-lu-ti-ya
to Nineveh, the city of my lordship.

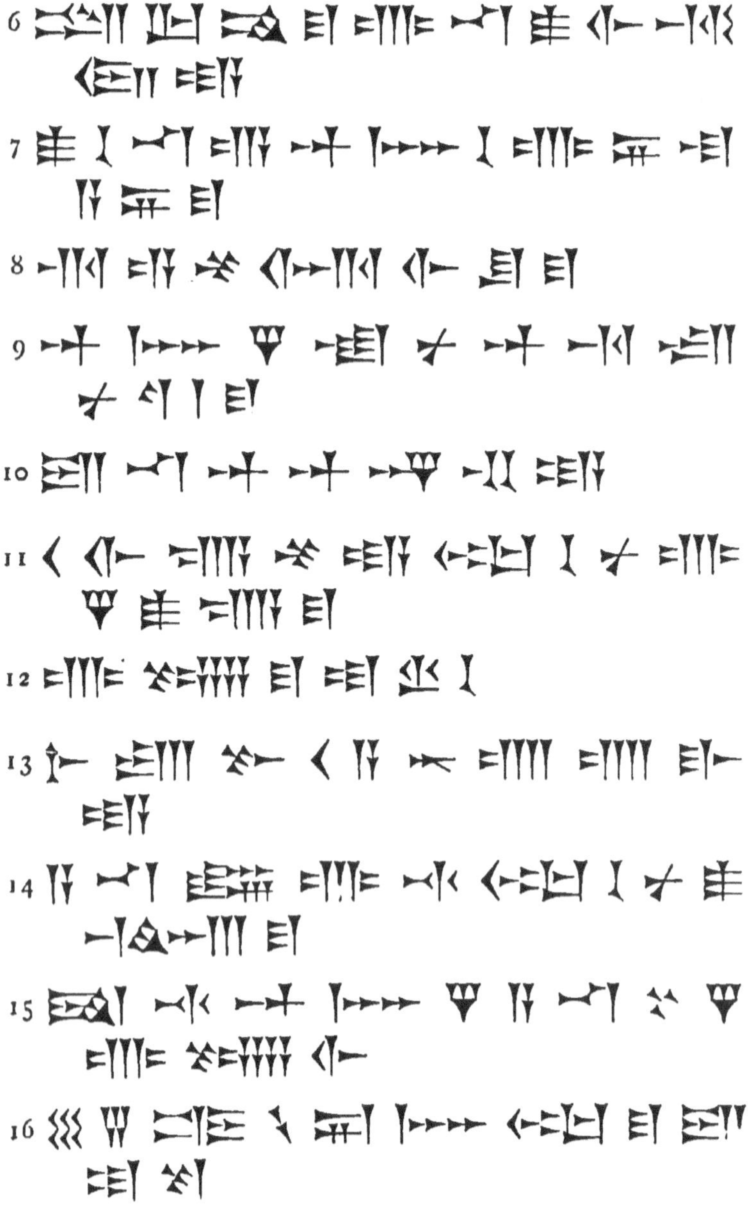

6 il-lic-av-va yu-na-as-si-ik SEPĀ-ya
he came and he kissed my two feet,

7 as-su na-dan ILI-su yu-tsal-la-a-ni-va
when the gift of (*i.e.*, giving back) he supplicated of me. Then[1]

8 ri-e-mu ar-si-su-va
compassion I showed (to) him, and

9 ILI sa-tu-nu au-khu-śu-nu ud-dis-va
of these gods their injuries I repaired, and

10 da-na-an, D.P., ASSUR BIL-ya
the mighty (deeds) of the god Assur, my lord,

11 u si-dhir SUM-ya eli-su-nu u-sa-as-dhir-va
and the writing of my name upon them I caused to be written and,

12 u-tir-va ad-din-su
I restored and I gave (them) to him.

13 D.P., Ta-bu-u-a tar-bit E.GAL-ya
The woman Tabūa, one reared (in) my palace,

14 a-na SARR-u-ti eli-su-nu as-cun-va
to the sovereignty over them I established, and,

15 it-ti ILI-sa a-na MAT-sa u-tir-si
together with her gods, to her land I restored her.

16 LXV, D.P., Gam-mali eli ma-da-at-te
Sixty-five camels more than the tribute

[1] A similar story is told of Yautāh, son of Khazāil, in Smith's *Assur-banipal*, page 283.

17 [cuneiform]

18 [cuneiform]

19 [cuneiform]

20 [cuneiform]

21 [cuneiform]

22 [cuneiform]

23 [cuneiform]

24 [cuneiform]

25 [cuneiform]

26 [cuneiform]

27 [cuneiform]

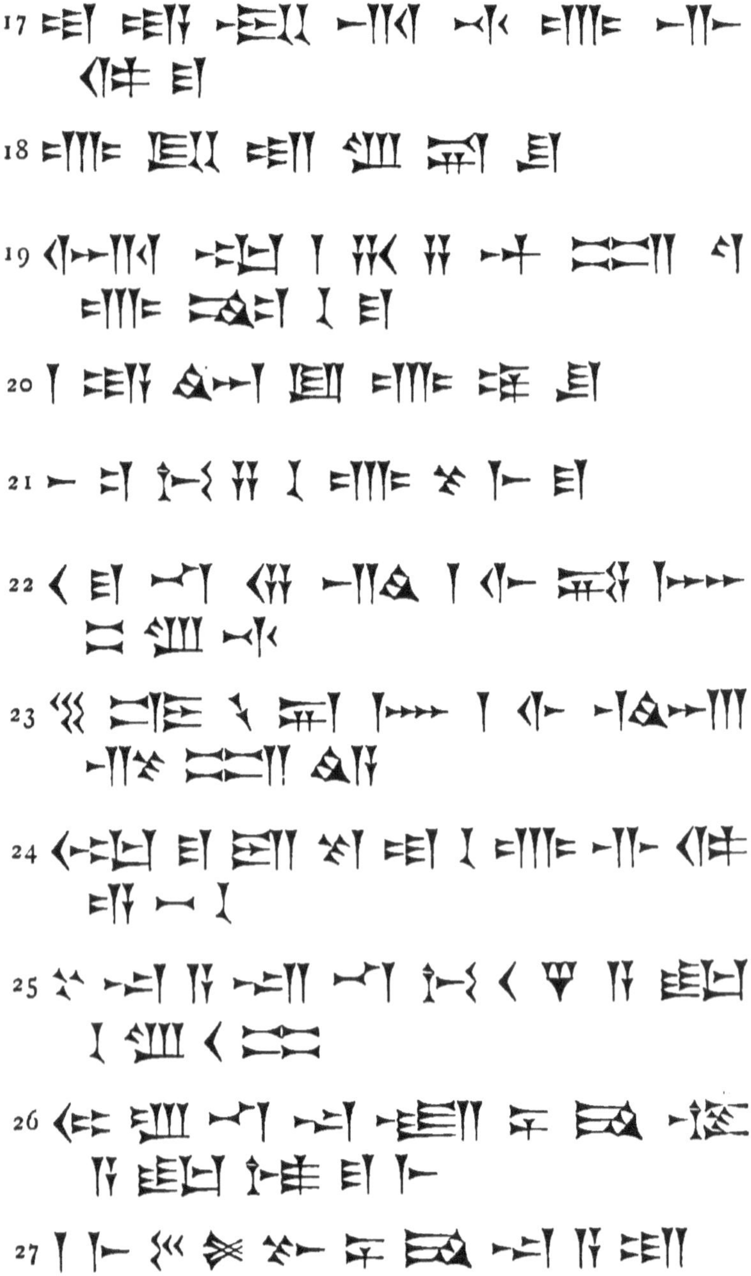

17 ABI-ya makh-ri-te u-rad-di-va
(paid to) my father in former times I added, and

18 u-cin tsi-ru-us-su
I placed upon him (her).

19 ar-ca, D.P., Kha-za-il sim-tu yu-bil-su-va
Afterwards Khazail, a plague carried him off, and

20 D.P., Ya-ah-lu-u ABIL-su
Yāhlu, his son,

21 ina, D.A., GU-ZA (cuśśu) su u-se-sib-va
upon his throne I caused to be seated; and

22 X. ma-na KHURATSU, I × 1000 ABNI bi-ru-ti
ten manehs of gold, one thousand carved stones,

23 L., D.P., gam-mali, I + 1000 GUN-ZI-RIK mahduti
fifty camels, one thousand *dromedaries*,

24 eli ma-da-te ABI-su u-rad-di e-mid-su
more than the tribute of his father I added, I appointed him

25 MAT Ba-a-zu na-gu-u sa a-sar-su ru-u-ku
the country of Bazu, a district of which its situation (is) remote,

26 mi-lac na-ba-li kak-kar MUNI a-sar tsu-ma-me
a journey of desert-land, a land of loathsomeness, a place of thirst,

27 I. + 100 × 40 CAS-BU kak-kar ba-a-tsi
one hundred and forty *casbu* of ground, dusty

28 
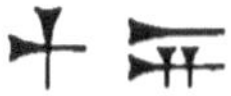 (*W.A.I.* iii., 15, 12.)

29 

30  [1]

31 

32  [2]

33 

34 

35 

36 

37 

[1]  *W.A.I.*, iii. 15, 13.

[2]  *nagû suatu*, "that district," is inserted after *e-ti-ik*, by *W.A.I.* iii. 15, 16.

28 pu-kut-tu u ABNI ca-za-bi-ti (*var.* ca-bar-ni)
broken (?), and stones deceitful (great (?). Heb. כבר).

29 XX. CAS-BU kak-kar TSIR u AKRABI
twenty kasbu of ground (where) snakes and scorpions

30 sa ci-ma zir-ba-bi ma-lu-u u-ga-ru (*var.* a-gar)
which, like grasshoppers, they filled the ground.

31 XX. CAS-BU MAT Kha-zu-u SAD-di, D.P., SAG-GIL-MUT
Twenty *kasbu* of the land of Khazu, a mountain of SAGIL-MUT stone,

32 a-na ARCI-ya u-vaś-śir-va e-ti-ik (*var.* na-gu-u su-a-tu)
behind me I left, and I passed through that district,

33 sa ul-tu YU-me ul-lu-ti
(into) which, from ancient times (days),

34 la il-li-cu SARRU pa-ni makh-ri-ya
had not marched (any) king preceding me.

35 Ina ci-bit, D.P., ASSUR, BIL-ya,
By the command of Assur, my lord,

36 ina cir-bi-su sal-dha-nis at-tal-lac
within it royally I marched.

37 SAMNA SARRANI sa ci-rib na-gi-e su-a-tu
Eight kings, which (were) within that district,

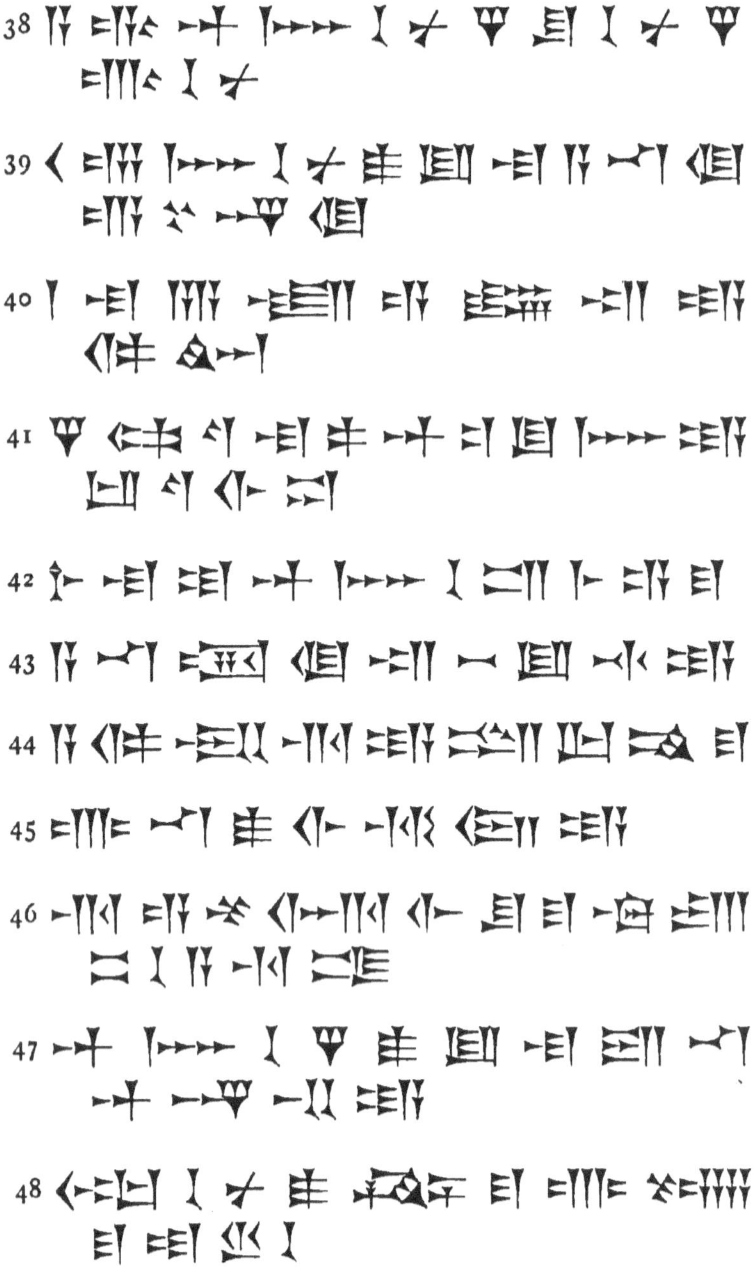
38
39
40
41
42
43
44
45
46
47
48

38 a-duc ILI-su-nu BUSU-su-nu NAMCUR-su-nu
I slew; their gods, their wealth, their riches

39 u NISI-su-nu as-lu-la a-na ci-rib MAT ASSUR, D.A.,
and their men I spoiled. To the interior of the land of Assyria,

40 D.P., La-ai-li-e SAR, D.P., Ya-di-ah
Lāilie, king of the city of Yadiah,

41 sa ul-tu la-pa-an, D.P., CACCI-ya ip-par-si-du
which from before my weapons had fled,

42 sal-la-at ILI-su is-me-e-va
of the spoiling of his gods he heard, and

43 a-na NINUA., D.A., AL be-lu-ti-ya
to Nineveh, the city of my lordship,

44 a-di makh-ri-ya il-lic-av-va
to my presence he came, and

45 yu-na-as-si-ik SEPĀ-ya
he kissed my two feet.

46 ri-e-mu ar-si-su-va ak-ta-bi-su a-khu-tuv
Compassion I showed him, and I spoke to him of brotherhood;

47 ILI-su sa as-lu-la da-na-an, D.P., ASSUR BIL-ya
(on) his gods which I had carried off (spoiled) the mighty (deeds) of Assur my lord

48 eli-su-nu as-dhur-va u-tir-va ad-din-su
upon them I wrote, and I restored (them) and I gave (them) to him.

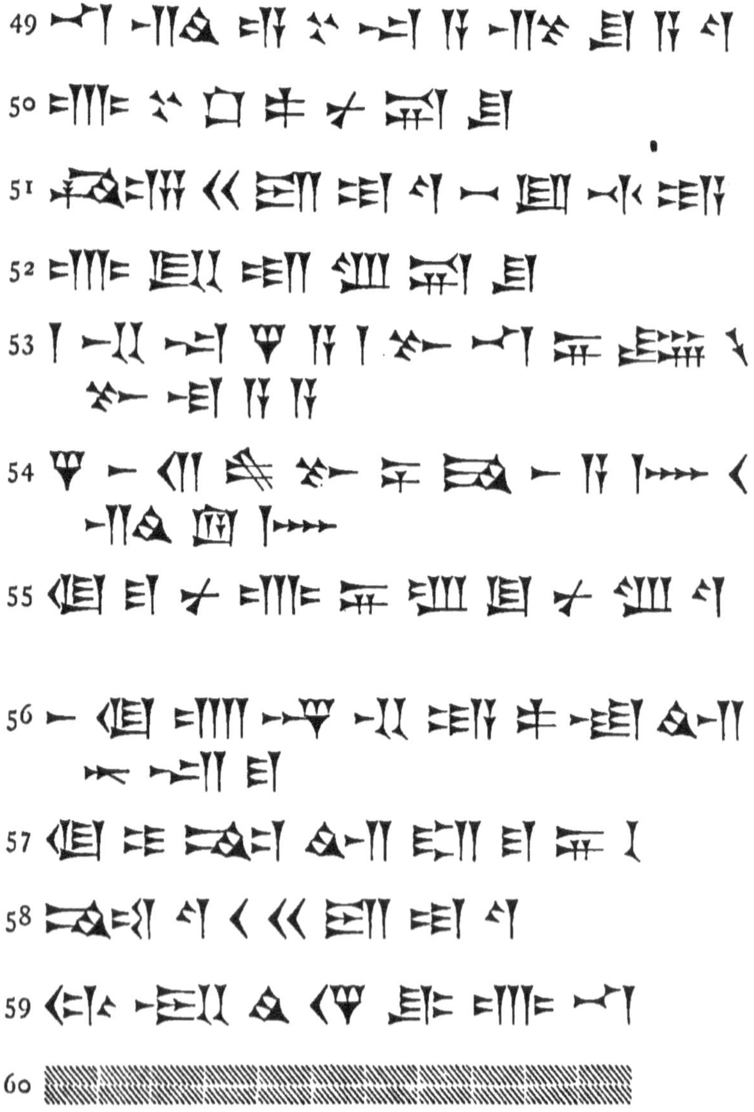

49 na-gi-e, D.P., Ba-a-zi su-a-tu
The districts of this land of Bāzu

50 u-sat-gil pa-nu-us-su
I caused to be entrusted to him,

51 BILAT (TIG-UN) man-da-at-tu bi-lu-ti-ya
offering (and) tribute to my lordship

52 u-cin tsi-ru-us-su
I fixed upon him,

53 D.P., BEL-ba-sa ABIL, D.P., Bu-na-ni SAR Gam-bu-la-ai
Bel-basa, son of Bunani, king of the Gambulāi

54 sa ina XII KAS-BU kak-kar ina MIE u KANI TSUTSI
who over twelve *kasbu* of ground among the waters and reedy marshes

55 ci-ma nu-u-ni sit-cu-nu sub-tav
like a fish (fishes) they were establishing their dwelling-place (seat).

56 Ina ci-bit ASSUR BIL-ya khat-tu ina-khats-zu-va
By the command of Assur, my lord, terror shook him and

57 ci-i dhe-im ra-ma-ni-su
according to his own decree

58 BILTU (TIG-UN) u man-da-at-tu
offering and tribute

59 ALPU makh-khi suk-lul sam-na
great ox(en) *complete? eight?*

60 . . . .
. . . .

THE WAR AGAINST SIDIR-PĀRNA AND EPĀRNA, KINGS OF MEDIA.

W.A.I., i. 46; col. iv.

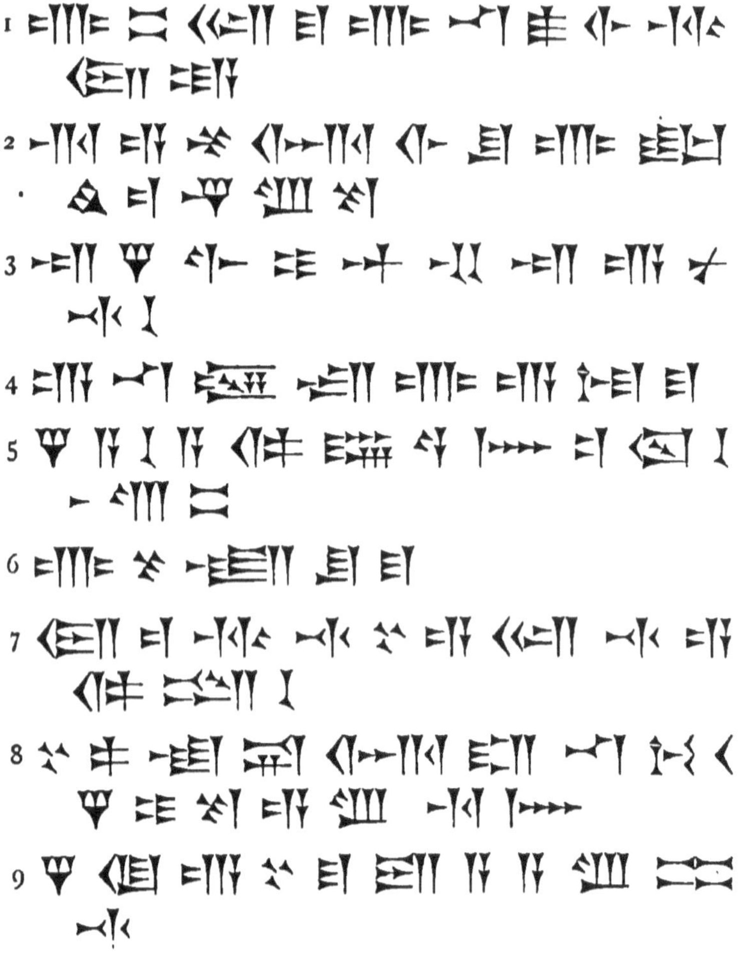

THE WAR AGAINST SIDIR-PĀRNA AND EPĀRNA, KINGS OF MEDIA.

W.A.I., i. 46; col. iv.

1 u-bi-lav-va yu-na-as-si-ik SEPĀ-ya
he brought and he kissed my feet,

2 ri-e-mu ar-si-su-va u-sar-khi-its sur-ru-te
compassion I showed him, and I caused to be washed away his rebellion.

3 D.P., Sa-pi-i, D.P., BEL AL dan-nu-ti-su
The city of Sapi-Bel, the city of his strength (*i.e.* stronghold),

4 dan-na-aś-śu u-dan-nin-va
its strength (fortification) I strengthened and

5 sa-a-su a-di, D.P., TSABI, D.P., MITPANI-su ina lib-bi
he himself, together with his bowmen (*lit.* bow-soldiers) within (it),

6 u-se-li-su-va
I made him go up and

7 CIMA, D.P., DAL-ti MAT E-lam-ti e-dhi-il-su
like a door, the land of Elam I shut it up.

8 MAT Pa-tu-us-ar-ra na-gu-u sa i-te-e-ru ITSTSURI
The land of Patūsarra a district from which the birds return,

9 sa ci-rib MAT Ma-da-ai ru-ku-ti
which (is) within the land of the Medes afar off (and)

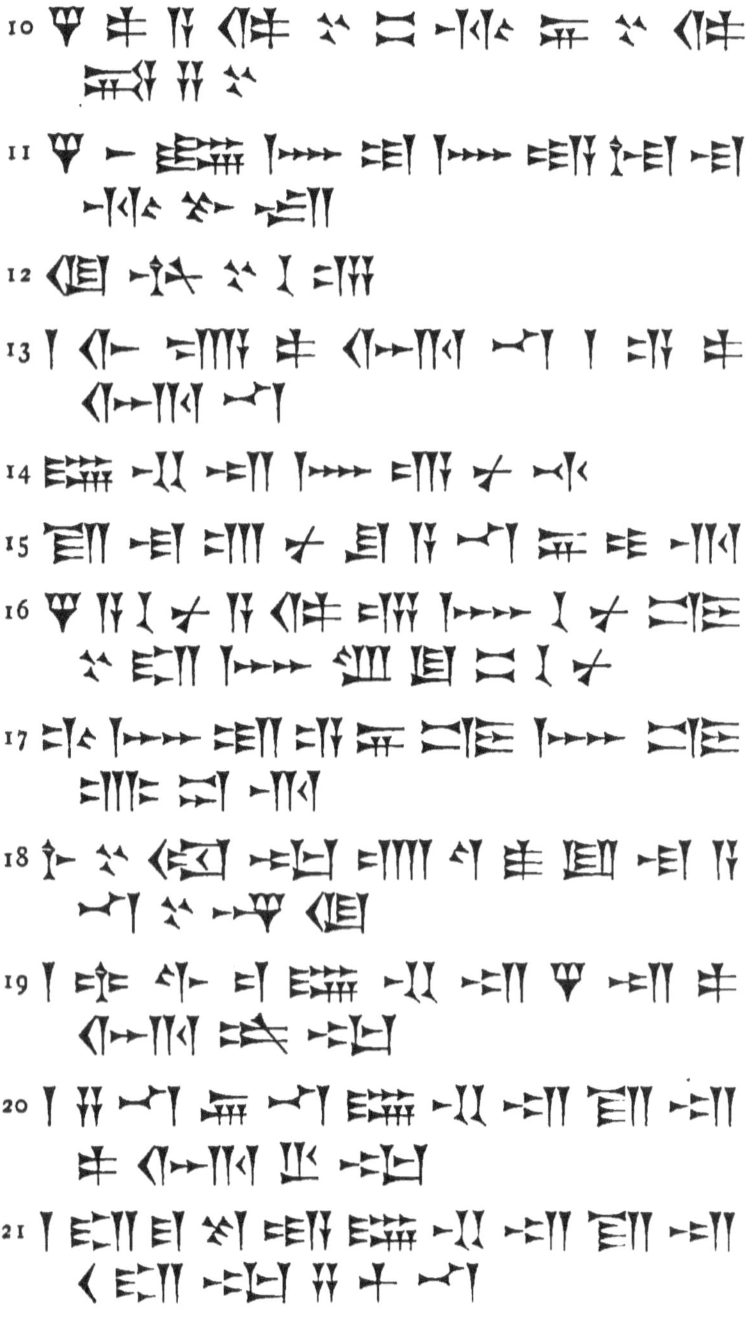

10 sa pa-a-di MAT Bi-ic-ni SAD-di, D.P., UCNI
which (is on) the borders of the land of Bicni, the mountains of marble (crystal)

11 sa ina SARRANI ABI-ya MIMMA la ic-bu-śu
which (land) among the kings, my fathers, none had trod

12 IRTSI-tiv MAT su-un
the territory of their country

13 D.P., Si-dir-pa-ar-na, D.P., E-pa-ar-na
Sidir-pārna (and) Epārna

14 D.P., BELI ALANI dan-nu-ti
the lords of the powerful cities

15 sa la-cit-nu-su a-na ni-i-ri
who had not submitted to my yoke

16 sa-a-su-nu a-di NISI-su-nu, D.P., śuśi ru-cu-bi-su-nu
they themselves together with their men, (their) horses, their chariots,

17 ALPI tsi-e-ni IMIRI, D.P., u-du-ri
oxen, sheep, asses, flocks,

18 sal-lat-sun ca-bit-tu as-lu-la a-na MAT ASSUR, D.A.,
their great spoil I carried off (spoiled) to the land of Assyria.

19 D.P., Uppits, D.P., BIL ALI sa, D.P., Pa-ar-tac-ca
Uppits, lord of the city of Pārtacca

20 D.P., Za-na-śa-na, D.P., BIL ALI sa, D.P., Pa-ar-duc-ca
Zanaśana, lord of the city of Pārtacca,

21 D.P., Ra-ma-te-ya, D.P., BIL ALI sa U-ra-ca-za-bar-na
Ramateya lord of the city of Uracazabarna

22 

23 

24 

25 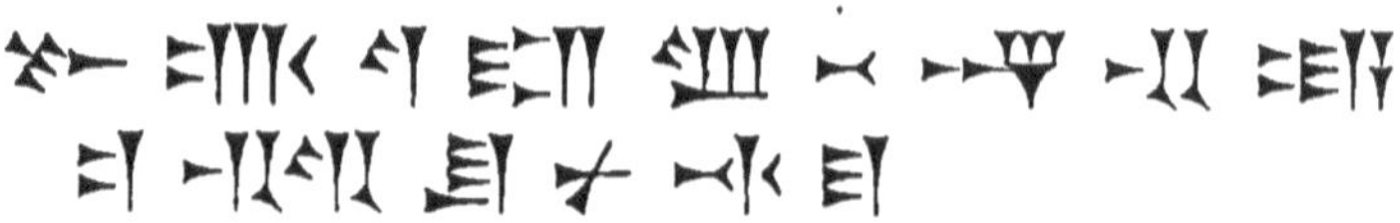

26 

27 

28 

29 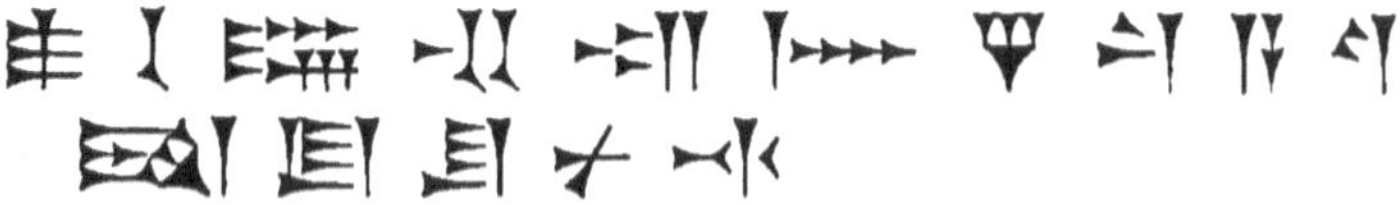

30 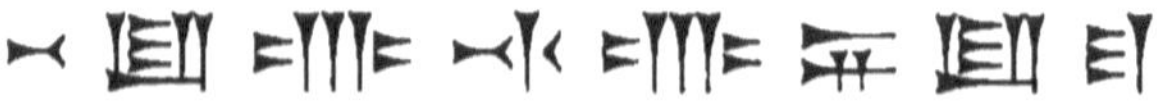

31 

32 

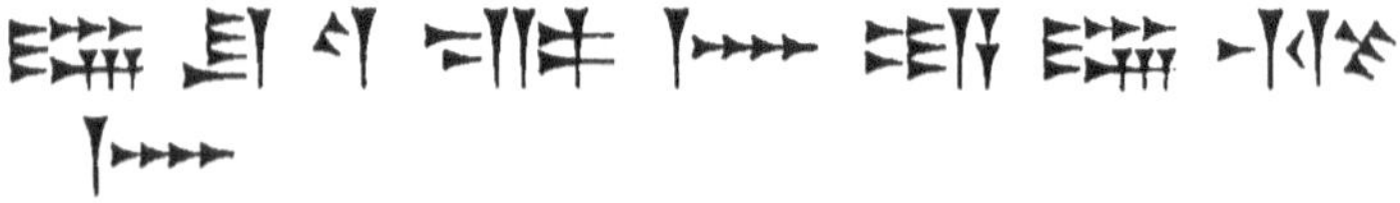

33 

22 MAT Ma-da-ai sa a-sar-su-nu ru-u-ku
(chiefs) of the country of the Medes, whose territory (is) afar off.

23 sa ina tar-tsi SARRANI ABI-ya IRTSI-tiv MAT ASSUR, D.A.
(Those chiefs) who in the time of the kings, my fathers, (to) the country of Assyria

24 la ip-pal-ci-tu-niv-va la-ic-bu-śu kak-kar-sa
had not crossed over, neither had they trodden its soil.

25 pu-lukh-tu ra-ru-bat ASSUR BIL-ya iś-khup-su-nu-ti-va
The fear (and) terror of the god Assur my lord overwhelmed them and

26 D.P., mur-ni-iś-ci RABI, D.P., UCNI dhi-ib MAT-su
great war horses, (and) choice marble of his land

27 a-na NINUA, D.A., AL be-lu-ti-ya
to Nineveh, the city of my lordship

28 is-su-niv-va yu-na-as-si-ku SEPĀ-ya
they had brought, and they kissed my two feet.

29 as-su, D.P., BILI ALANI sa ka-a-tav id-cu-su-nu-ti
As regards the lords of cities who (my) hands had struck them,

30 be-lu-u-ti yu-tsal-lu-va
my lordship they implored and

31 e-ri-su-in-ni cit-ru
they asked of me a treaty.

32 D.P., SU-PAR-SAKI-ya, D.P., PIKHATI
My officers, the prefects

33 sa pa-a-di MAT su-un
of the borders of their country

34 

35 

36 

37 

38 

39 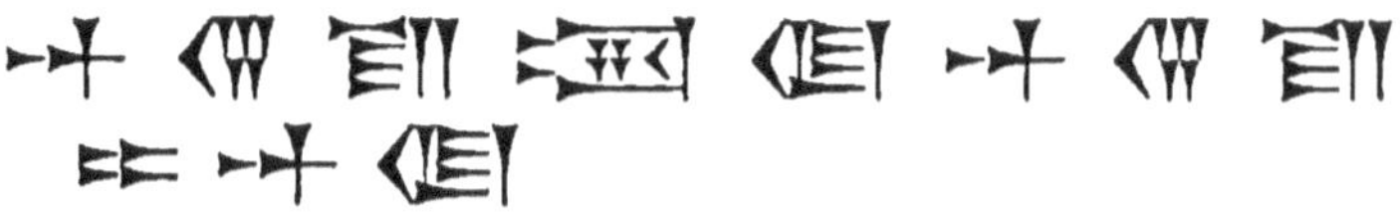

40 

41 

42 

43 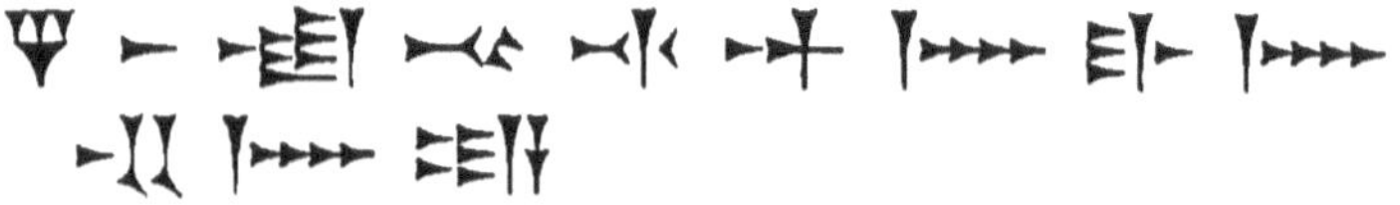

44 

34 it-ti-su-nu u-ma-ah-ir-va
with them I urged on and

35 NISI a-si-bu-ut ALANI sa-tu-nu
the men, inhabitants of those cities,

36 ic-bu-śu-va yu-sac-nis-su SEPÁ-us-su-un
they trampled (upon) and they made to submit to their feet

37 BILAT (TIG-UN) man-da-tu be-lu-ti-ya sat-ti sam-ma iv-cin tsi-ru-su-un
offering (and) tribute to my lordship, yearly the sum, I fixed upon them.

38 Ul-tu, D.P., ASSUR, D.P., SAMAS, D.P., BELU u, D.P., NABU
From (the time when) the gods Assur, Samas, Bel, and Nebo

39 D.P., ISTAR sa NINUA, D.A., D.P., ISTAR sa ARBA-il, D.A.
The goddess Istar of Nineveh, the goddess Istar of Arbela

40 eli na-ci-ri-ya ina li-i-ti
over my enemies by the law (which)

41 yu-sa-zi-zu-ni am-tsu-u ma-la lib-bi-ya
they had caused to fix for me, I found the fulness (of the desire) of my heart.

42 ina ci-sit-ti na-ci-ri sat(?) lu-u-ti
By the acquisitions from enemies (?)

43 sa ina tu-gul-ti ILI RABI BELI-ya
which in the service of the great gods my lords

44 ik-su-da ka-ta-ai
my two hands have captured.

THE BUILDINGS OF ESARHADDON.

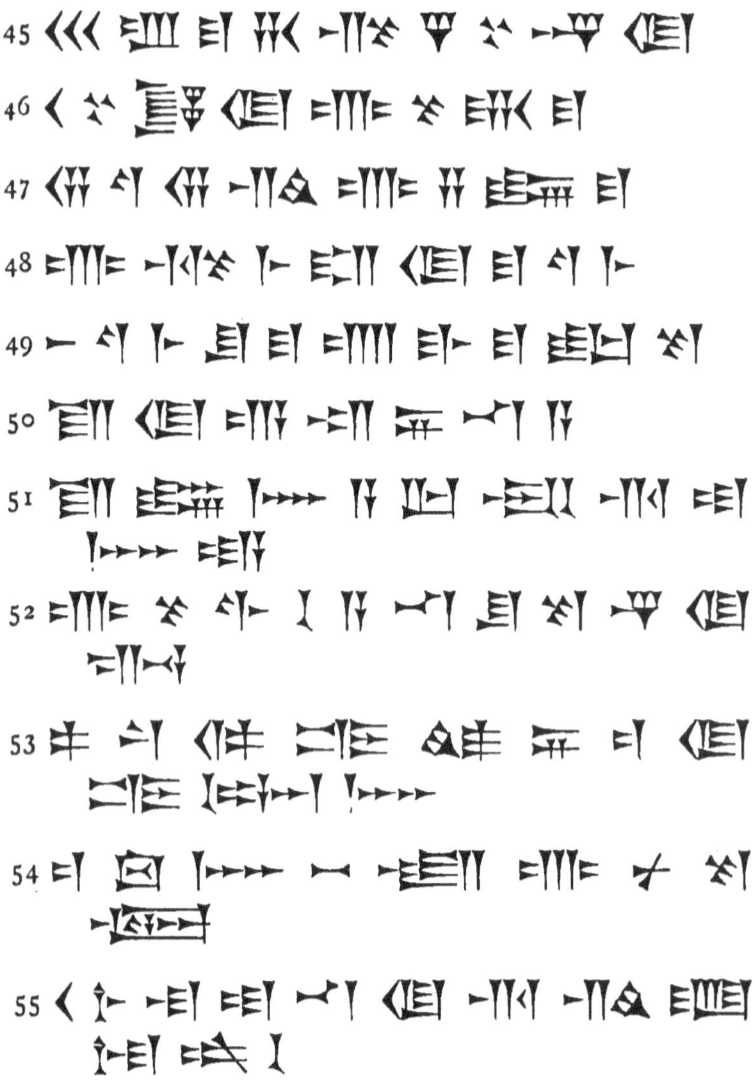

THE BUILDINGS OF ESARHADDON.

45 es-rit ma-kha-zi sa MAT ASSUR, D.A.
Ten strongholds of the land of Assyria

46 u MAT ACCAD, D.A., u-se-pis-va
and the land of Accad I caused to be made, and

47 CAŚPU KHURATSU u-za-in-va
(with) silver (and) gold I decorated, and

48 u-nam-me-ra ci-ma YU-me
I made brilliant as the day (light).

49 Ina YU-me-su-va E-GAL ma-khir-te
At that time also the principal palace

50 sa ci-rib, D.P., Ni-na-a
which (is) within the city Nineveh

51 sa SARRANI a-lic makh-ri ABI-ya
which the preceding kings, my fathers,

52 yu-se-pi-su a-na su-te-sur CARASI
they caused to be made for the custody of the camp-baggage

53 pa-ka-di, D.P., mur-ni-iś-ci, D.P., PARRATI
(and) the oversight of the war horses, cows (mules),

54 D.P., RUCUBI bat-li u-nu-te TAKHATSI
chariots, arms, the furniture of battle,

55 u sal-la-at na-ci-ri gi-mir NIN-SUM-su
and the spoil of enemies, all (of it) whatever its name.

56 

57 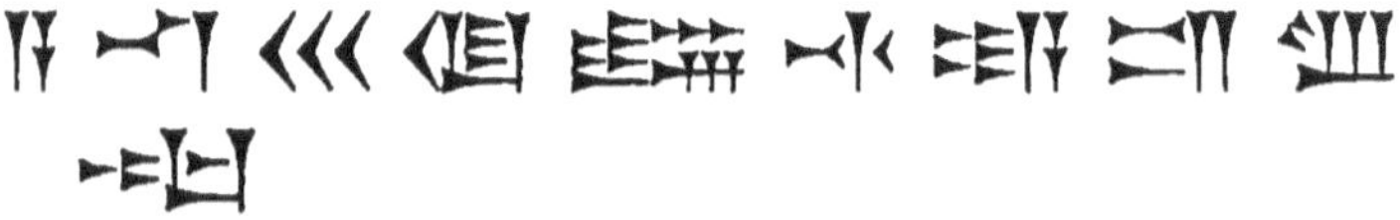

58 

59 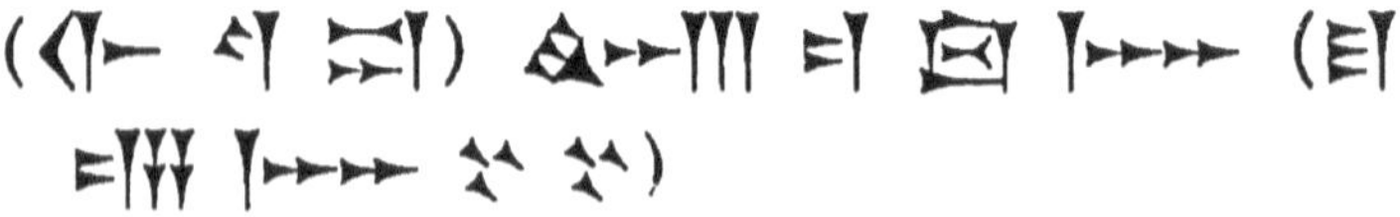

THE BUILDING OF THE PALACE.

W.A.I., i. 47; col. 5.

1 

2 

3 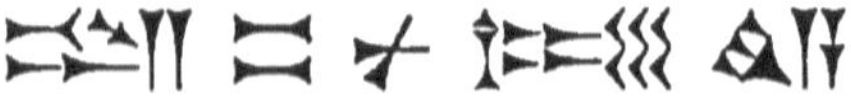

4 

5 

56 sa, D.P., ASSUR SAR ILI
Which the god Assur, the King of gods

57 a-na es-ci SARRU-ti-ya is-ru-ca
to the *hand?* of my kingship hath granted

58 (a-na sit)-cin, D.P., śuśi
for the establishment of horses,

59 (si-par-du)-ukh, D.P., RUCUBI (va NISI MATATI)[1]
(?) of chariots and the men of the countries

THE BUILDING OF THE PALACE.

W.A.I., i. 47; col. 5.

1 (sa ak-ta)-sad se-ci-bu ina, D.P., MITPANI-ya
which I captured ravishing with my bow

2 ma-al-lu mus-sic-cu u-sa-as-si-su-nu-ti-va
full tax(es) I caused them to bear and

3 il-bi-nu LABINI[2] MAHDI
they made many bricks.

4 E-GAL TSAKH-ra su-a-tu
That small palace

5 a-na śi-khi-ir-ti-sa ag-gur-va
to its whole extent I dug up and

[1] The text of the transliteration in brackets, in lines 58 and 59, is restored from *W.A.I.*, iii. 16, 6.

[2] Compare לִלְבֹּן הַלְּבֵנִים, Exodus v. 7.

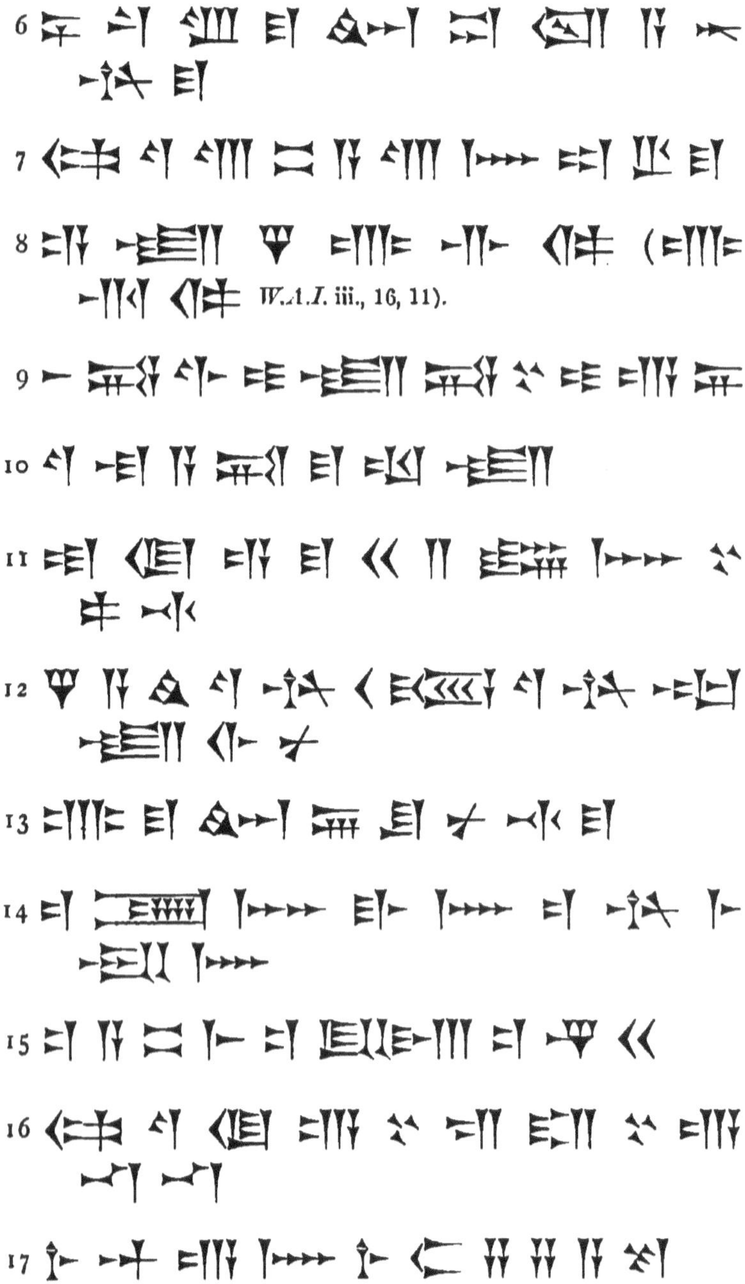
6
7
8
W.A.I. iii., 16, 11).
9
10
11
12
13
14
15
16
17

6 kak-ka-ru ma-ah-du CIMA a-sil TIM-MA
much earth like the line of a rope

7 ul-tu lib-bi ECILI ab-duk-va
from the interior of the lands I dug and

8 e-li-sa u-rad-di (*var.* u-ri-di)
upon it, I added; (and)

9 ina D.P., pi-i-li ABNU SAD-i dan-ni
with alabaster a stone from the great mountain

10 tu-la-a us-ma-al-li
the mound I filled up

11 ad-ci-e-va 20 + 2 SARRANI MAT khat-ti
I gathered, and twenty-two kings of the land of the Hittites

12 sa a-khi tam-tiv u GABAL tam-tiv ca-li-su-nu
of the sea-coast and the middle of the sea, the whole of them

13 u-ma-ah-ir-su-nu-ti-va
I hastened them on and

14 D.P., GUSURI RABI, D.P., tim-me RABI
great beams (for) a great floor (of)

15 D.P., A-bi-me, D.P., ERINU, D.P., SUR-MAN
Abime wood, cedar wood, sherbin wood

16 ul-tu ci-rib MAT S'i-ra-ra MAT Lib-na-na
from the interior of the land of S'irara (and) the land of Lebanon,

17 SAL LAMAŚŚI sal-lat tsa-tsa-a-te
sphinxes (female colossi) and a height of statuary work

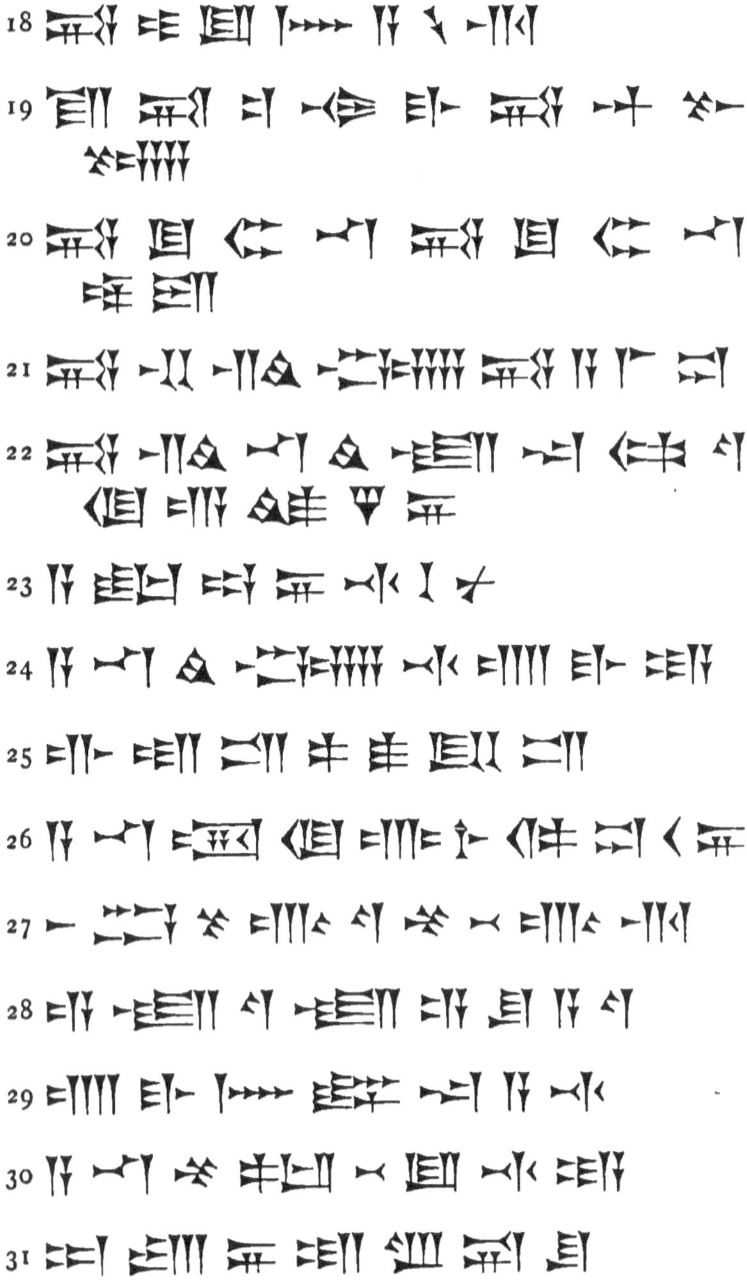

18 D.P., AZKUPPATI a-gur-ri
door posts of burnt brick,

19 sa, D.P., SAMULLU, D.P. . . . .
of Samulla stone (alabaster) . . . . . stone,

20 D.P., CU-MI-NA, D.P., CU-MI-NA TUR-DA
Cumina stone, strong Cumina stone

21 D.P. . . . . D.P., A-LAL-DU
. . . . . stone . . . . . stone

22 D.P., GI-NA-KHI-GUB-BA ul-tu ci-rib khar-sa-ni
. . . . stone from the interior of the forests,

23 a-sar nab-ni-ti-su-nu
the place of their production,

24 a-na khi-sakh-ti E-GAL-ya
for the requirements of my palace,

25 mar-tsi-is pa-as-ki-is
laboriously (and) with difficulty

26 a-na NINUA, D.A., yu-sal-di-du-u-ni
to Nineveh they had caused to be brought.

27 Ina ARKHU SEGA MAGARU YU-mu mit-ga-ri
In a fortunate month (on) a favourable day,

28 e-li tu-li-e su-a-tu
upon that mound,

29 HECALI rab-ba-a-ti
great palaces

30 a-na mu-sab be-lu-ti-ya
for the dwelling of my lordship

31 ab-ta-ni tsi-ru-us-su
I built upon it.

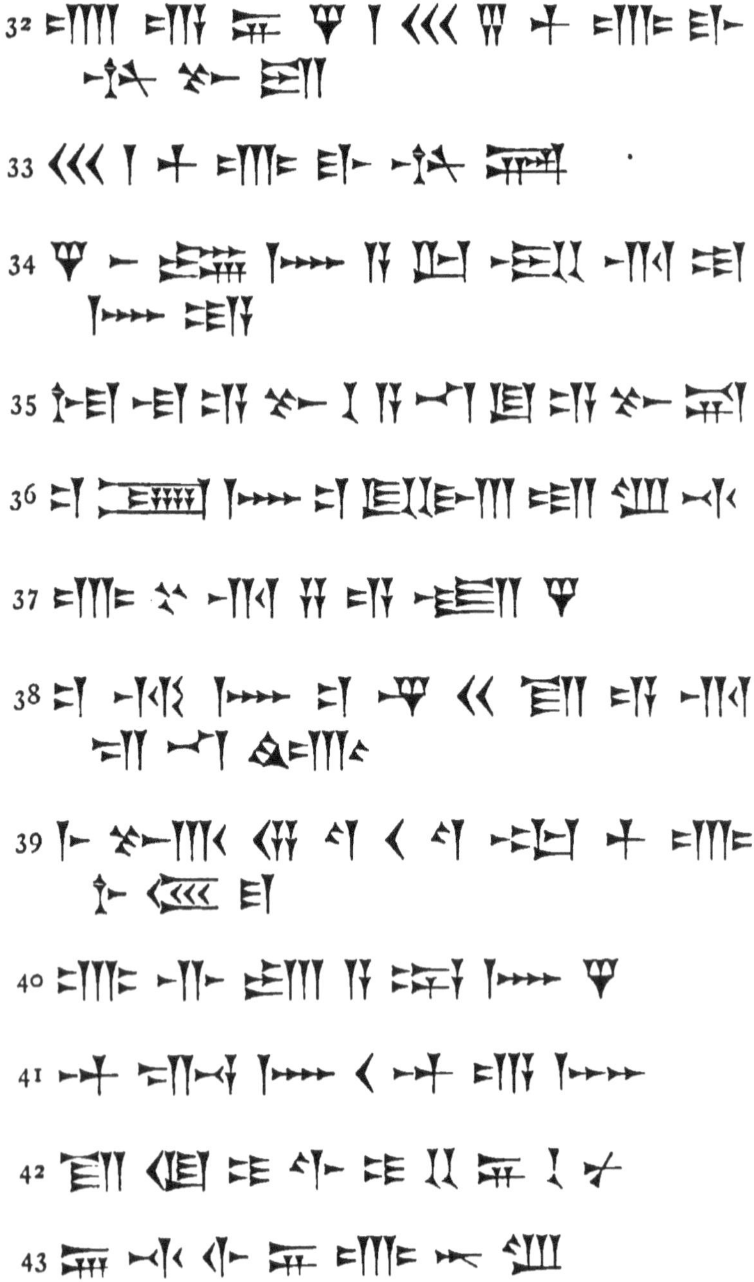

32 BITU dan-ni sa SUSSU + SILASÂ + KHAMSA bar-u rab-tiv sadadu
A strong temple of ninety-five great *baru* in length,

33 SILASÂ + I bar-u rab-tiv RAPASTU
Thirty-one great baru in width,

34 sa ina SARRANI a-lic makh-ri ABI-ya
which among the preceding kings, my fathers,

35 MIMMA la-e-pu-su a-na-cu e-pu-us
any one (of them) had not made, I made.

36 D.P., GUSURI, D.P., ERINU tsi-ru-tu,
Beams of cedar, great

37 u-sat-ri-tsa e-li-sa
I caused to be placed upon it.

38 D.P., DALTI, D.P., sur-man sa e-ri-śi-na DHABU
Doors of Sherbin wood, of which their foundation (is) good,

39 me-śir CAŚPU u ŚIPARRU u-rac-ciś-va
a band of silver and copper I bound (on them), and

40 u-rat-ta-a BABI-sa
I hung in its gates

41 SEDI u LAMAŚŚI
bulls and colośśi,

42 sa ci-i pi-i sic-ni-su-nu
who, according to their fixed command,

43 ir-ti lim-ni yu-tar-ru
against the wicked they turn (themselves);

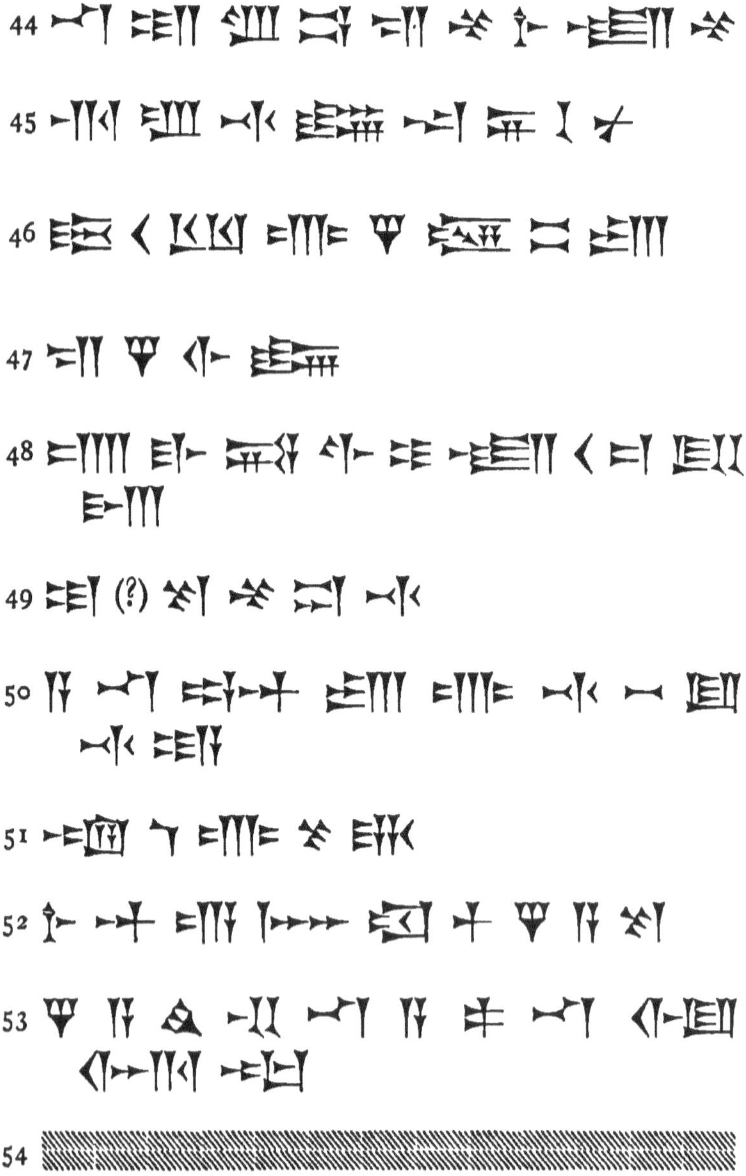

44 na-tsi-ru cip-śi mu-sal-li-mu
they protect the footsteps, making peace

45 tal-lac-ti SAR ba-ni-su-nu
(to be upon) the path of the King, their creator (who made them).

46 IMNU u SUMELU u-sa-ats-bi-ta
(Positions) to the right hand and left I caused to take (occupy)

47 śi-gar-si-ui
the avenue of them.

48 E-GAL, D.P., pi-i-li u, D.P., ERINI
A palace of alabaster and of cedar wood

49 at (?) te mu-du-ti
. . . . (?) . . . .

50 a-na mul-ta-u-ti be-lu-ti-ya
for the renown of my lordship

51 nac-lis u-se-pis
completely I caused to be made.

52 sal LAMASSI ERI mas-sa-a-te
Female colossi of painted (?) bronze,

53 sa a-khi-en-na-a pa-na va (ar-ca)
which (were) on this side, in front and behind, (I raised).

54 . . . . [1]
. . . .

[1] The cylinder containing this inscription is broken here, but another line is evidently wanted to complete the sentence.

W.A.I., i. 47 ; col. 6.

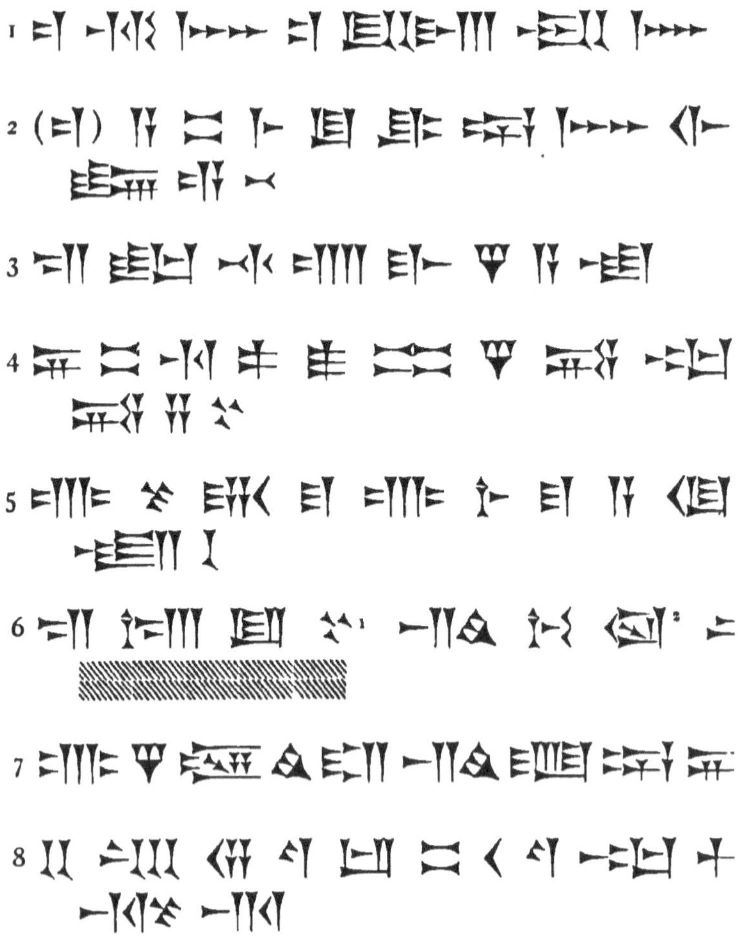

¹ Var. 

² Mr. Norris inserts (*Dict.*, p. 1057) the two signs  after *cima*, but I have been unable to find the tablet which gave this reading.

W.A.I., i. 47 ; col. 6.

1 D.P., DALTI, D.P., ERINU RABI,
The doors of great (planks) of cedar wood,

2 (D.P.) A-bi-me cu-lul BABI-si-in e-mid
of Abime wood, the completion of the gates I placed (made).

3 śi-khar-ti E-GAL sa-a-tu
The whole extent of that palace,

4 ni-bi-khu pa-as-ku sa, D.P., CA, D.P., UCNI
a battlement (?) broken of eye-stone (and) marble (crystal)

5 u-se-pis-va u-sal-ma-a RISATUV-su
I caused to be made, and I completed its summit,

6 śi-el-lu-lat gi-gu CIMA . . . .
stairs of the roof like . . . .

7 u-sa-aś-khi-ra gi-mir BABANI
I caused to surround all the doors

8 śic-cat CAŚPU ib-bu u ŚIPARRU nam-ri
coverings of white silver and shining copper (and),

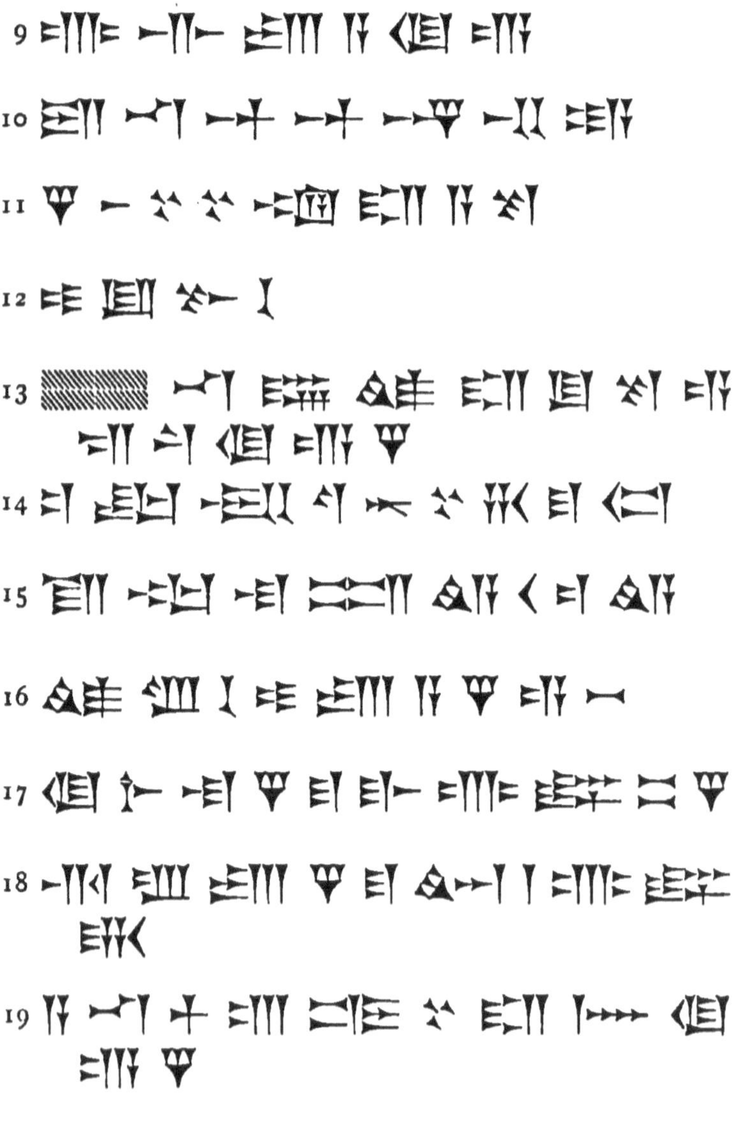

9 u-rat-ta-a ci-rib
I hung (them) within (it).

10 da-na-an, D.P., ASSUR BIL-ya
The mightiness of the god Assur my lord

11 sa ina MATATI nac-ra-a-te
(with) which in hostile lands

12 i-lu-bu-su
he had clothed himself,

13 . . . . na, D.P., khar-ra-cu-te e-śi-ka ci-rib-sa
priests (?) I established (?) within it.

14 D.P., CIRU RABU taṁ-sil MAT kha-ma niv[1]
A great plantation like (that) of the land of Amanus,

15 sa ca-la SIM MAHDU U ETS(I) MAHDU
which (contained) all spices and tree(s),

16 khar-ru-su i-ta-a-sa e-mid
its ditch, its walls, I made to stand;

17 ci-sal-la-sa ma-rab u-rab-bi-va
its altar in size I made large, and

18 tal-lac-ta-sa ma-ah-dis u-rab-bis
its paths greatly I enlarged

19 a-na mas-cit, D.P., ŚUŚI ci-rib-sa
for the reception of horses within it.

[1] A similar act is recorded of Tiglath-Pileser I., B.C. 1130, in *W.A.I.*, i. 15, 16–27, where it is said, "The cedar, the *liccarina* tree and the almug, from the countries I have conquered, these trees which none of the kings, my fathers, that were before me, had planted, I took, and in the plantations of my land I planted, and by the name of plantation I called them; whatsoever there was not in my land I took (and) the plantations of Assyria I established."

20 [cuneiform]

21 [cuneiform]

22 [cuneiform]

23 [cuneiform]

24 [cuneiform]

25 [cuneiform]

26 [cuneiform]

27 [cuneiform]

28 [cuneiform]

29 [cuneiform]

30 [cuneiform]

31 [cuneiform]

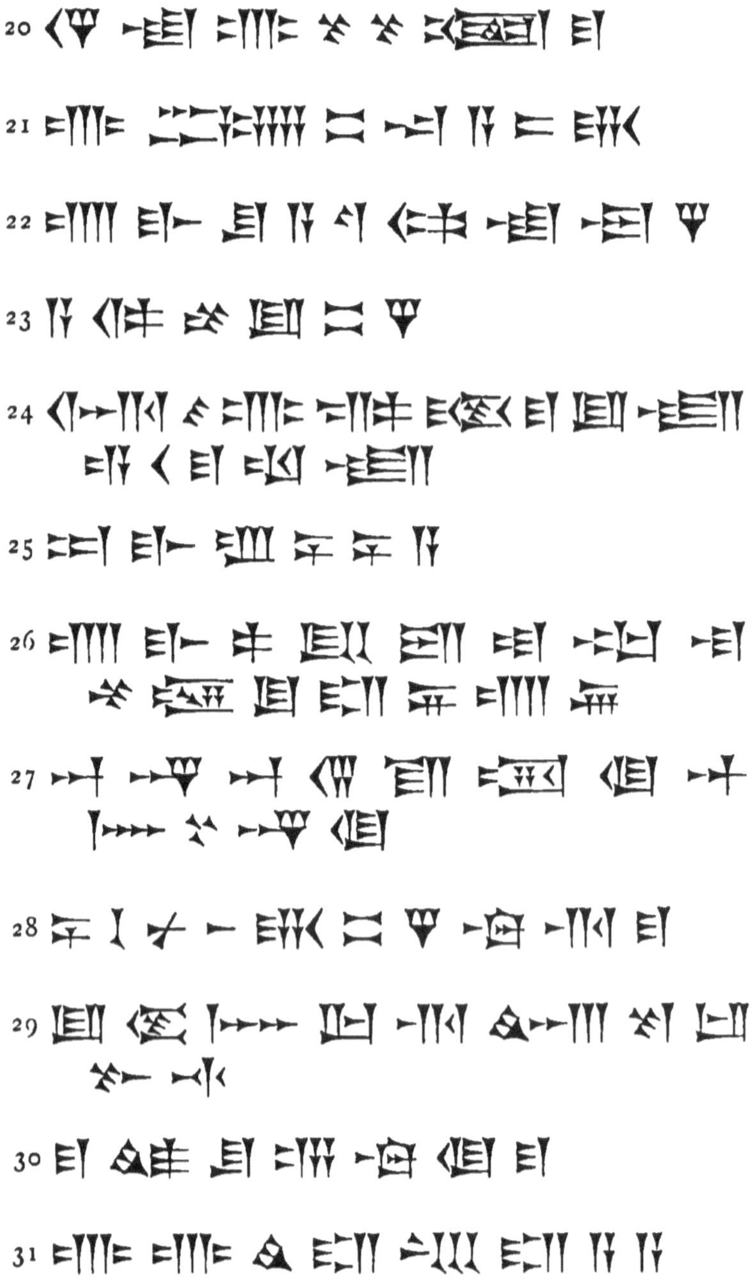

20 pat-tu u-se-se-rav-va
An opening I caused to make straight, and

21 u-sakh-bi-ba-a dhab-bis
I caused to . . . . . beautifully

22 E-GAL su-a-tu ul-tu USSI-sa
that palace from its foundation

23 a-di takh-lu-bi-sa
to its roof.

24 ar-tsip u-sac-lil-va lu-li-e u-ma-al-li
I built, I caused to be finished, and with fulness I filled (it);

25 ES-GAL . . . . EPUS-a
(also) the great gate . . . . . I made.

26 E-GAL pa-ki-da-at ca-la-mu az-cu-ra ni-bit-śa
The palace of the oversight of the world, I recorded (called) its name.

27 D.P., ASSUR, D.P., ISTAR sa NINUA, D.A., ILI MAT ASSUR, D.A.
The god Assur, the goddess Istar of Nineveh, the gods of the land of Assyria,

28 CALI-su-nu ina kir-bi-sa ak-ri-va
the whole of them within it I summoned, and

29 D.P., NIKI ur-ri-ikh-te ib-bu-ti
victims plentiful, (speedy) pure,

30 ma-khar-su-un ac-ci-va
before them I sacrificed, and

31 u-sam-khi-ra cat-ra-ai
I caused to present my peace offerings.

32 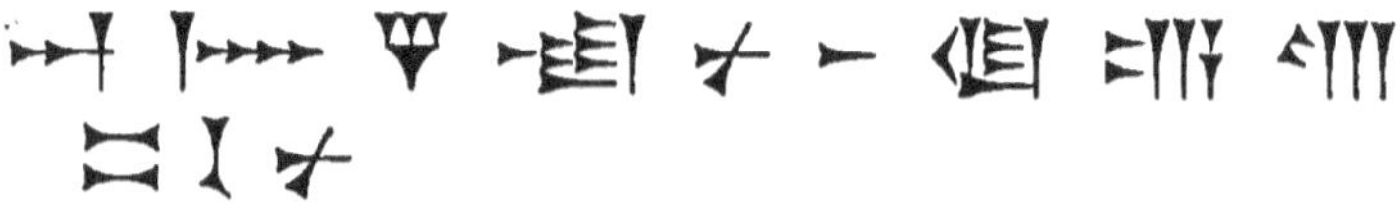

33 

34 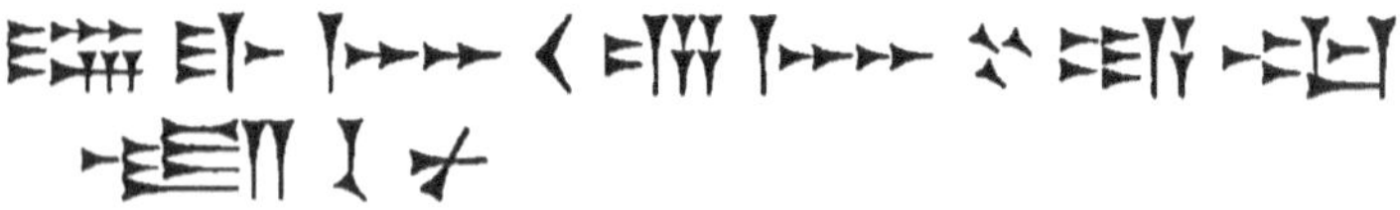

35 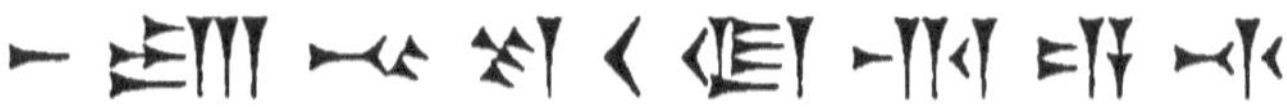

36 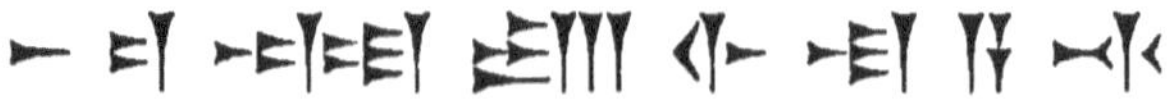

37 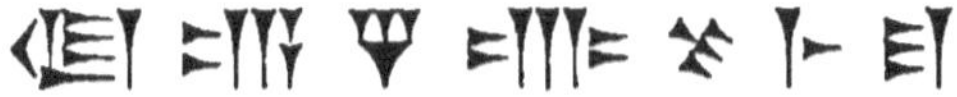

38 

39 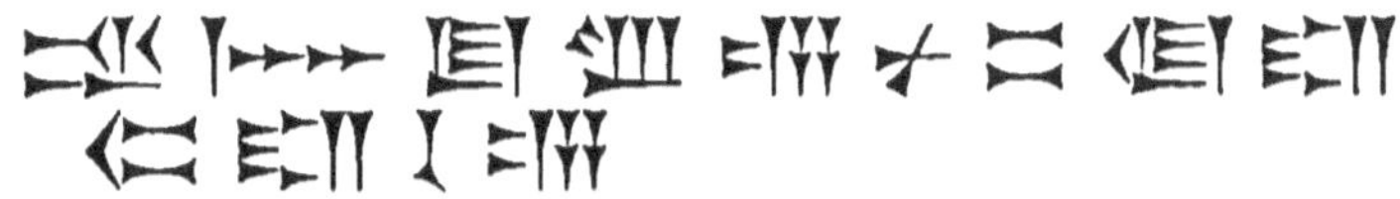

40 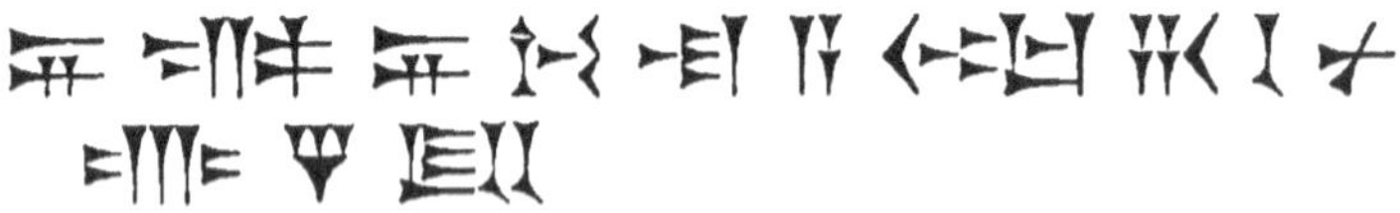

41 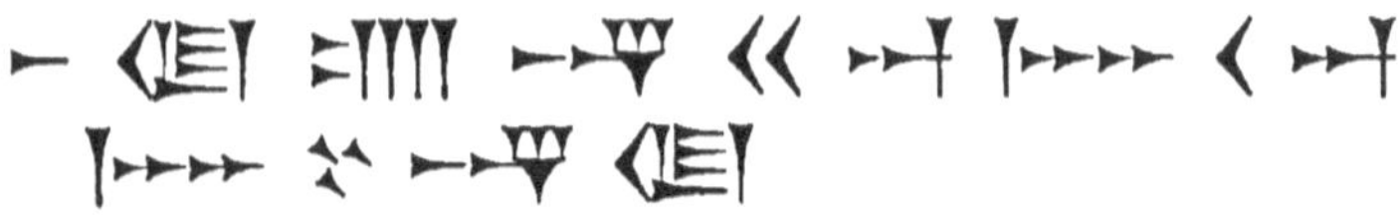

32 ILI sa-tu-nu ina ci-rib lib-bi-su-nu
Those gods in the interior of their hearts

33 ik-tar-ra-bu SARR-u-ti
approached my kingdom.

34 D.P., RABI u NISI MAT-ya ca-li-su-nu
The chiefs and men of my land, the whole of them,

35 ina ta-gul-te u ci-ri-e-ti
in service and homage

36 ina is-sik-ta si-la-a-ti
with submission, peaceful

37 ci-rib-sa u-se-sib-va
within it I caused to be seated, and

38 u-sa-li-za nu-par su-un
I caused to be glad their soul.

39 CARANI cu-ru-un-nu bi-ci-ra tsur-ra-su-un
Grape wine[1] ? ?

40 ni-sak-ni gu-la-a mukh-kha-su-nu u-sa-cin
(as tribute ?) upon them I established.

41 Ina ci-bit ASSUR SAR ILI u ILI MAT ASSUR, D.A.
By the command of Assur, King of the gods, and the gods of the land of Assyria

[1] The names of five sorts of wines are given by a bi-lingual list in *W.A.I.*, ii. 44, 9-13. In *W.A.I.*, i. 65, 22, we read,—*caranuv mat Izällav mat Tuahimmu mat Tsimmini mat Khibuniv mat Aranabaniv mat 'Sūtsav mat Bit-Cubativ mat Bitātiv cima mē nāri la nabīv ina, D.P., passaru, D.P., Marduk va, D.P., Tsirpanituv beli-a lu udāssiv.* "Wines from the countries of Izallav, Tuahimmu, Tsiminni, Khibuniv, Aranabaniv, Sutsav, Beth-Cubativ, Bitativ, like river waters (in quantity) without number in the bowl of Marduk and Tirpanituv, my lords, then I poured out."

42 [cuneiform]

43 [cuneiform]

44 [cuneiform]

45 [cuneiform]

46 [cuneiform] (var. [cuneiform]) [cuneiform]

47 [cuneiform] ([cuneiform]) [cuneiform]

48 [cuneiform]
(var. [cuneiform]) (W.A.I. iii., 16, 8.)

49 [cuneiform]

50 [cuneiform]

51 [cuneiform]

52 [cuneiform]

[1] [cuneiform] (W.A.I., iii. 16, 3).
[2] Var. [cuneiform].

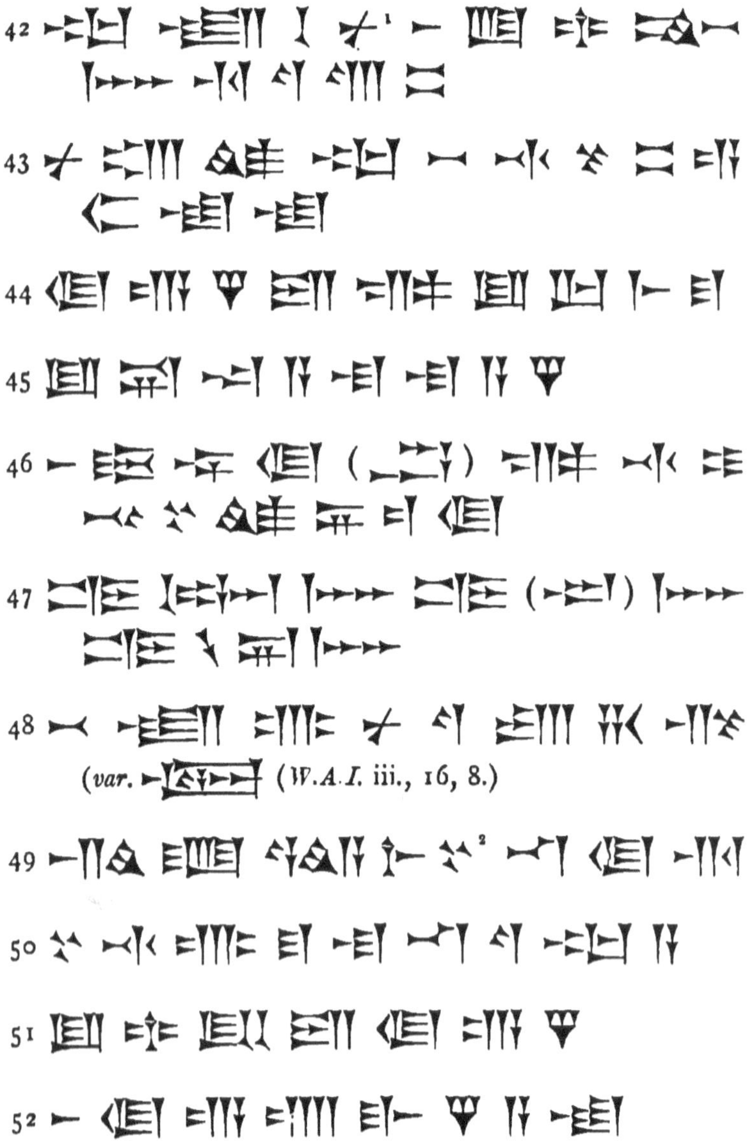

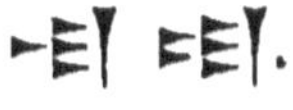

42 ca-li-su-nu (*var.* CALI-su-nu) ina dhu-ub SERI khu-ut lib-bi
all of them in health of limbs, joy of heart,

43 nu-um-mur ca-bat-ti se-bi-e lit-tu-ti
lightness of liver, abundance of offspring,

44 ci-rib-sa da-ris lu-tas-sib-va
within it, eternally, mayest thou dwell, and

45 lu-us-ba-a la-la-a-sa
may its fulness be abundant.

46 ina SUMELI muk-ki ARKHU ris-ti-i cul-lat mur-ni-is-ci
At the left hand of the building (in), the first month, all the war horses,

47 D.P., PARRATI IMIRI[1] D.P., gam-mali
cows (mules), asses, camels,

48 bat-li u-nu-ut ta-kha-zi
arms, the furniture for war,

49 gi-mir UMMANI sal-lat (*var.* la-at) na-ci-ri
the whole army (and), the spoil of enemies,

50 sat-ti sam-ma la na-par-ka-a
yearly, a sum unbroken,

51 lu-up-ki da ci-rib-sa
then I appointed (to be) within it.

52 Ina ci-rib E-GAL-sa-a-tu
In the interior of that palace

[1] Omitted by the text in *W.A.I.*, iii. 16, 8.

53 

54 

55 

Concluding Passage from *W.A.I.*, iii. 16.

British Museum, No. 11 $\frac{48}{315}$ 4.

56 

57 

58 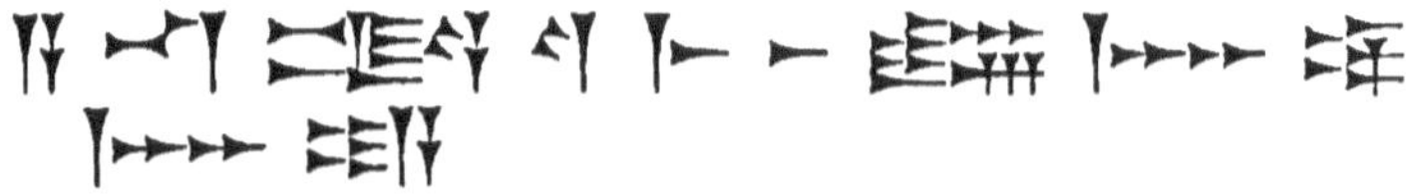

59 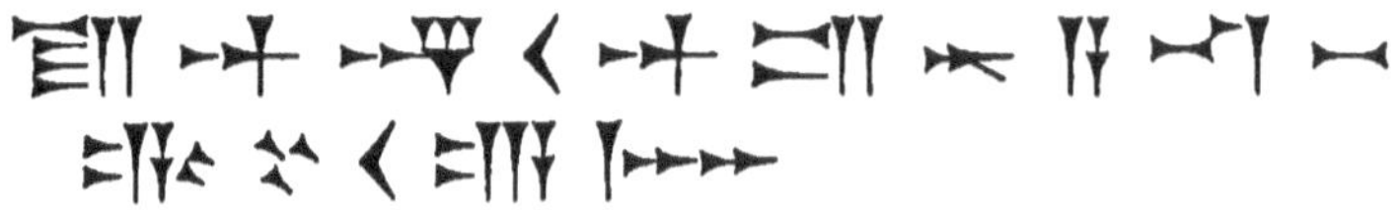

60 

61 

62 

53 SEDU DAMKU la-maś-śi DAMKU
a propitious bull, a propitious colossus

54 na-tsir cip-śi SARRU-ti-ya
the protector(s) of the footsteps of my kingship

55 mu-kha-du-u ca-bat-ti-ya[1]
rejoicing my liver.

Concluding Passage from *W.A.I.*, iii. 16.

British Museum, No. $11\frac{48}{315}4$.

56 da-ris lis-tap-ru-u
eternally may they send (me)

57 ai ip-par-ku-u i-da-a-sa
may its walls not be broken (down).

58 a-na ARCAT YU-me ina SARRANI ABLI-ya
For a future day (for which ever king) among the kings my sons

59 sa, D.P., ASSUR u, D.P., ISTAR a-na be-lut MAT u NISI
whom the god Assur, and the goddess Istar to the government of the land and people

60 i-nam-bu-u zi-cir-su
shall proclaim his name.

61 e-nu-va E-GAL sa-a-tu
when this palace

62 i-lab-bi-ru-va i-na-khu
shall grow old and shall decay.

[1] The cylinder from which the previous text has been taken ends here, and the following lines are added from the broken cylinder, but they are lithographed in *W.A.I.*, i. 47, as if they were a part of the other text.

63 

64 

65 

66 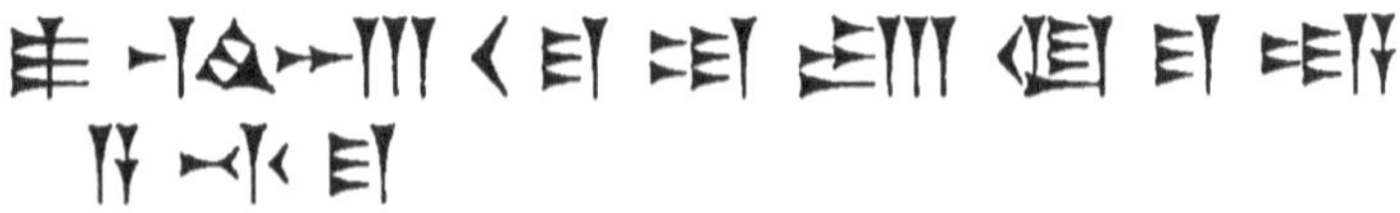

67 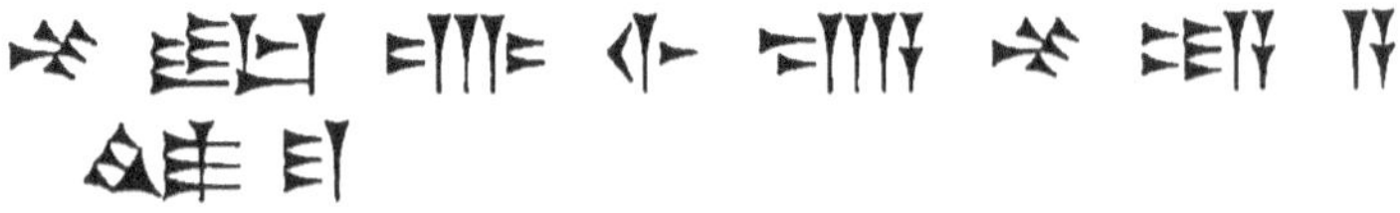

68 

69 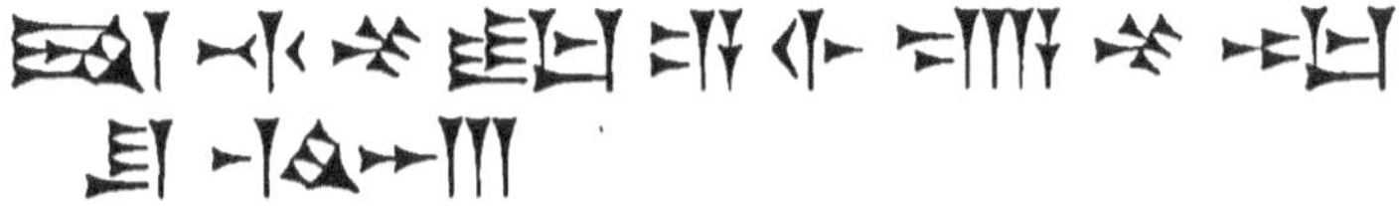

70 

71 

Date from *W.A.I.*, i. 47.

Date from *W.A.I.*, iii. 16–24.

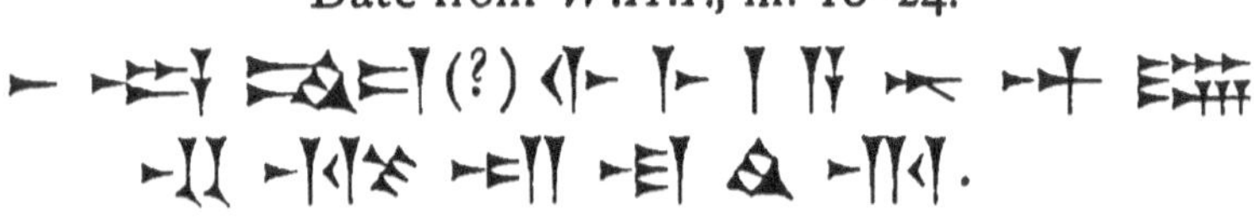

63 an-khu-uś-śa lu-(ud)-dis
Its ruins may he renew (repair)

64 ci-i sa a-na-cu mu-sa-ru-u si-dhir
even as I the straight line of writing of

65 SUM SARI ABU ba-ni-ya it-ti mu-sar-e si-dhir SUM-ya
the name of the king, my father, my begetter, with the straight lines of the writing of my name,

66 as-cun-u-va at-ta ci-ma ya-a-ti-va
have established, (so do) thou like myself also

67 mu-sar-u si-dhir SUM-ya a-mur-va
the written writing of my name see and

68 CIŚALLU bu-su-us, D.P., NIKU NA-ci
the altar cleanse, a victim sacrifice

69 it-ti mu-sar-e si-dhir SUM-ca su-cun
with the written writing thy name place

70 D.P., ASSUR va, D.P., Is-tar
the god Assur, and the goddess Istar

71 ik-ri-bi-ca i-sim-mu-u
thy prayers (then) shall hear.

Date from *W.A.I.*, i. 47.

Ina ARAKH AB YUMU xviiith . . . . . .
(Dated) in the month AB (July) 18th day . . . . . .

Date from *W.A.I.*, iii. 16–24.

Ina ARAKH AB (?) lim-me, D.P., A-KHAZ-EL, D.P., BILU PIKHATU, D.P., La-khi-ri
(Dated) in the month AB, eponym Ahazel, the lord prefect of the city Lakhiri.

THE NAMES OF THE EIGHT KINGS

(AND THEIR CITIES), TO WHICH REFERENCE IS MADE IN

Col. iii. 37.

W.A.I., iii. 15 ; Col. 4, 19-24.

19 〒 〈𒀭〉 𒈾 𒁹 𒊏 𒉡 〈𒆠 𒁹

〒 𒁉 𒈾 𒐈 𒊏 𒉡 𒊑 𒀭 𒅆 𒀀

20 〒 𒁺 𒈠 𒉺 𒈗 𒊏 𒁹 𒁹 𒅆 𒈠

𒀸 𒁹 𒈠 𒀀 𒁹 𒊏 𒉡 𒉡 𒁹

𒀀 𒁹 𒌋 𒅆 𒈠

21 〒 𒍑 𒉍 𒉡 𒊏 𒉡 𒁹 𒁹 𒉡

𒀀

〒 𒈠 𒍑 𒐈 𒊏 𒉡 𒈨 𒀀 𒈠

𒅆 𒈠

22 𒀸 𒁹 𒈨 𒁹 𒊏 𒉡 𒉡 𒈨 𒀭 𒁹

〒 𒍑 𒁹 𒅆 𒐈 𒊏 𒉡 𒊮 𒁹

𒀀

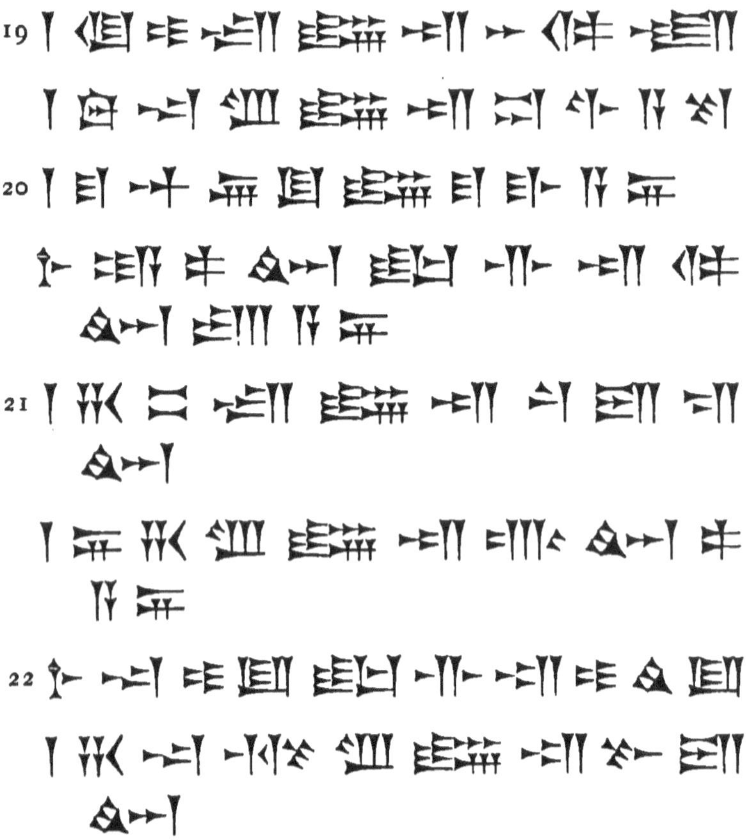

THE NAMES OF THE EIGHT KINGS

(AND THEIR CITIES), TO WHICH REFERENCE IS MADE IN

Col. iii. 37.

W.A.I., iii. 15; Col. 4, 19–24.

19 D.P., Ci-i-śu SAR, D.P., Khal-di-li
Ciśu, king of Khaldili;
D.P., Ak-ba-ru SAR, D.P., Du-pi-a-te
Akbar, king of Dupiate;

20 D.P., Ma-an-śa-cu SAR, D.P., Ma-gal-a-ni
Mānśacu, king of Magalani;
D.P., Ya-pa-ah sar-rat, D.P., Di-ah-ta-a-ni
Yapāh, queen of Diahtāni;

21 D.P., Kha-bi-śu SAR, D.P., Ka-da-śi-ah
Khabiśu, king of Kadaśiah;

D.P., Ni-kha-ru SAR, D.P., Ga-ah-pa-ni
Nikharu, king of Gāhpani;

22 D.P., Ba-i-lu sar-rat, D.P., I-khi-lu
Bailu, queen of Ikhilu;
D.P., Kha-ba-nam-ru SAR, D.P., Bu-da-ah
Khabanamru, king of Budāh;

23 

24 

THE NAMES OF THE TWENTY-TWO KINGS

(AND THEIR CITIES), TO WHICH REFERENCE IS MADE IN

Col. v. 12.

The following text is from *W.A.I.*, iii. 16; Col. 5, 12.

12 

13 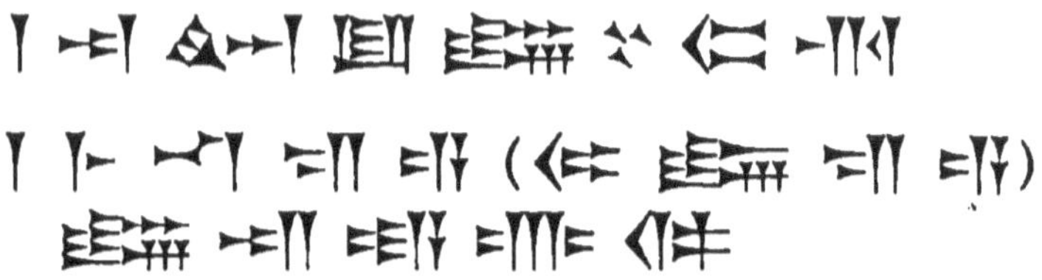

14 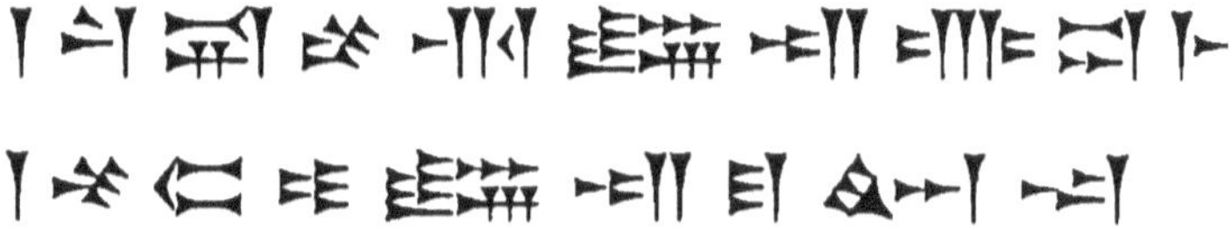

23 SAMNA SARRANI sa ci-rib na-gi-e su-a-tu a-duc
eight kings which (were) within those districts I slew:

24 ci-ma (a)-bu-bu as-ta-di pa-gar ku-ra-di-su-un
like a storm I destroyed. The dead bodies of their warriors, etc.

THE NAMES OF THE TWENTY-TWO KINGS

(AND THEIR CITIES), TO WHICH REFERENCE IS MADE IN

Col. v. 12.

The following text is from *W.A.I.*, iii. 16, 21. The script of the writing on the cylinder, from which the copy in *W.A.I.*, iii. 16–21 is made, is very much rubbed, and the differences in the names of the cities given below are caused by the comparison of them with an identical list found on a fragment of a broken cylinder of Assur-bani-pal.—R.M., 3.

12 ad-ci-e-va SARRANI MAT khat-ti u e-bir A-AB-BA
I assembled, and the kings of the Hittites and along (beyond) the sea (*viz.*)—

13 D.P., Ba-ah-lu SAR, D.P., Tsur-ri
Baal, king of Tyre;

D.P., Me-na-śi-e (*var.* Mi-in-śi-e) SAR, D.P., Ya-u-di
Menasseh, king of the city of Judah;

14 D.P., Ka-us-gab-ri SAR, D.P., U-du-me
Kausgabri, king of Edom;

D.P., Mu-tsur-i SAR, D.P., Ma-ah-ba
Mutsuri, king of Moab;

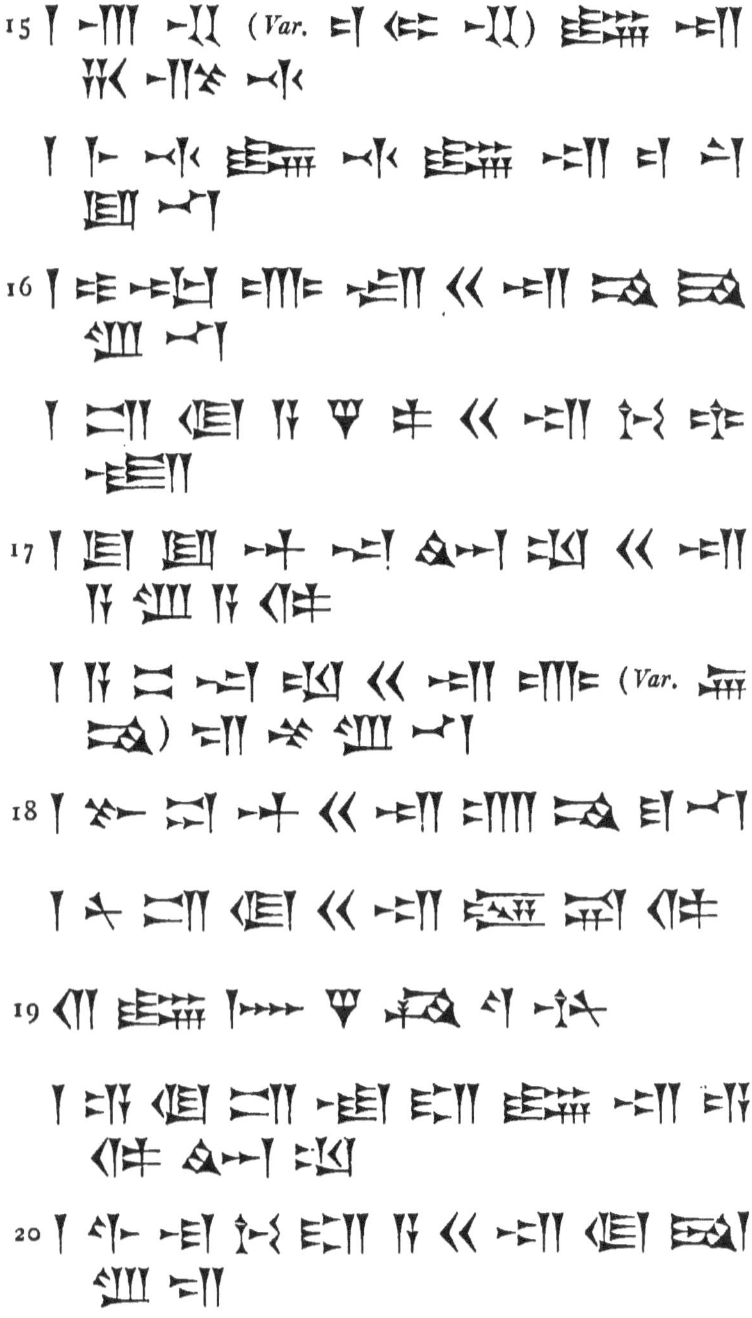

15 D.P., 'Sili-Bel SAR, D.P., Kha-zi-ti
Tsili-Bel, king of Gaza;

D.P., Me-ti-in-ti SAR, D.P., Is-ka-lu-na
Metinti, king of Askelon;

16 D.P., I-ca-u-śu SAR, D.P., Am-gar-ru-na
Icauśu, king of Ekron;

D.P., Mil-ci-a-sa-pa SAR, D.P., Gu-ub-li
Milciasapa, king of Gubli;

17 D.P., Cu-lu, D.P., Ba-ah-al SAR, D.P., A-ru-a-di
Culu-Baal, king of Arvad;

D.P., A-bi-Ba-al SAR, D.P., Sam (*var.* śa-am) śi-mu-ru-na
Abibaal, king of 'Samśimuruna;

18 D.P., Bu-du-il SAR, D.P., Bit-am-ma-na
Buduil, king of Beth-Ammon;

D.P., AKHI-mil-ci SAR, D.P., Ats-du-di
Akhimelec, king of Ashdod;

19 XII SARRANI sa CISAD tam-tiv
twelve kings of the neighbourhood of the sea.

D.P., E-ci-is-tu-ra SAR, D.P., E-di-ha-al
Ecīstura, king of Ediahal;

20 D.P., Pi-la-gu-ru-a SAR, D.P., Ci-id-ru-śi
Pylagoras, king of Cidruśi;

21 [cuneiform text]

[cuneiform text]

22 [cuneiform text]

[cuneiform text]

23 [cuneiform text]

24 [cuneiform text]

[cuneiform text]
(var. [cuneiform text])

25 [cuneiform text]

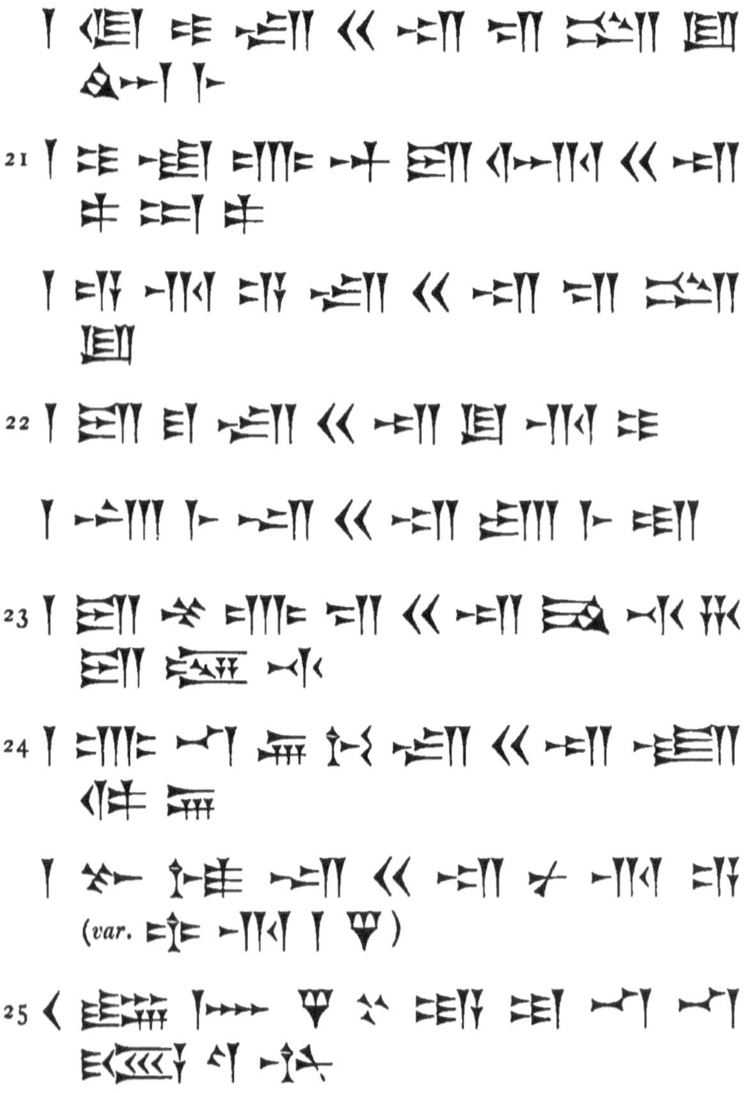

D.P., Ci-i-śu SAR, D.P., 'Si-il-lu-ah-me
Kissos, king of Salamis;

21 D.P., I-tu-u-an-da-ar SAR, D.P., Pa-ap-pa
Ithuander, king of Paphos;

D.P., E-ri-e-śu SAR, D.P., 'Si-il-lu
Eriesu, king of Soloi;

22 D.P., Da-ma-śu SAR, D.P., Cu-ri-i
Damaśu, king of Curi (Kurium);

D.P., Adh-me-zu SAR, D.P., Ta-me-tsi
Adhmezu (Admetus), king of Tametsi (Tamassus);

23 D.P., Da-mu-u-śi SAR, D.P., Gar[1]-ti-kha-da-ats-ti
Damūśi, king of Gartikhadatsti;

24 D.P., U-na-śa-gu-śu, SAR, D.P., Li-di-ir
Unaśaguśu, king of Lidir;

D.P., Bu-tsu-zu[2] SAR, D.P., Nu-ri-e
Butsuzu, king of Nurie;

25 X SARRANI sa MAT Ya-at-na-na KABAL tam-tiv
ten kings of the land of Cyprus in the middle of the sea.

[1] The first sign of the name given in Smith's "Assurbanipal," page 32, is , *am*, which "was compared to the Greek *Ammochosta*, and the modern *Famagosta* (see "Records of the Past," iii. 108).

[2] This king is called king of Up-ri-tis-sa (*W.A.I.*, iii. 27, 133), which has been compared to Aphrodisium.

26 

26 IN SUMMA XXII SARRANI MAT khat-ti a-khi tam-tiv GABAL tam-tiv CALI-su-nu

Altogether twenty-two kings of the country of the Hittites, the sea coast (and) the border of the sea, all of them.

THE EGYPTIAN CAMPAIGN OF ESARHADDON.

No notice or account of Esarhaddon's Egyptian campaign occurs on the large and nearly complete cylinder, a copy of which is printed in the preceding pages. Our knowledge of it is obtained from tablet fragments in the British Museum Collection and short notices in the "Annals of Assur-bani-pal." The two following are the principal annal notices (*W.A.I.*, iii. 17, 51-62):—

"In my first expedition to Makan and Meroë, then I went. Tirhakah, king of Egypt and Ethiopia, whose overthrow Esarhaddon, king of Assyria, the father, my begetter, had accomplished and had taken possession of his country; then he, Tirhakah, the might of the god Assur, the goddess Istar, and the great gods, my lords despised, and trusted to his own might . . . . . ; (59) and to capture Egypt he came against them, he entered and sat in Memphis, the city which the father, my begetter, had taken, and to the boundaries of Assyria had added."

W.A.I., iii. 28, 6–8.

"Tirhakah against the men of Assyria, who within Egypt (were) tributaries dependent on me whom Esarhaddon, king of Assyria, the father, my begetter, to kingdoms had appointed, in the midst of it came."

Egypt and Ethiopia were under the rule of Tirhakah during the first part of Esarhaddon's reign, but the latter drove him out of Egypt. In the latter part of Esarhaddon's reign Tirhakah again conquered Egypt, and this was probably the cause of Assur-bani-pal's expedition to that country.

NOTICE OF THE EGYPTIAN CAMPAIGN OF ESARHADDON BY HIS SON ASSUR-BANI-PAL.

Cylinder E, *W.A.I.*, iii. 29.

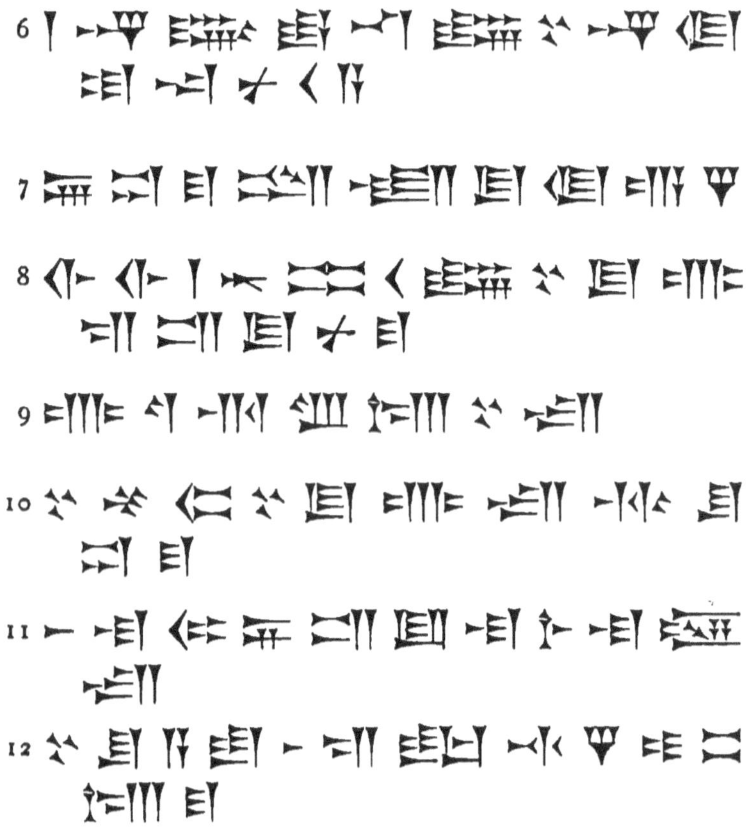

NOTICE OF ESARHADDON'S EGYPTIAN CAMPAIGN BY HIS SON ASSUR-BANI-PAL.

Cylinder E, *W.A.I.*, iii. 29.

6 D.P., ASSUR-AKHA-IDIN-na SAR MAT ASSUR, D.A., ba-nu-u-a
Esarhaddon, king of the land of Assyria, the father, my begetter,

7 ir-du-va il-li-cu ci-rib-sa
had descended and had marched into the midst of it.

8 ABICTA, D.P., Tar-ku-u SAR MAT Cu-u-śi is-cu-nu-va
The defeat of Tirhakah, king of the land of Ethiopia, he had established and

9 yu-par-ri-ru el-lat-śu
scattered his forces.

10 MAT mu-tsur MAT Cu-u-śi ik-su-da-va
The country of Egypt (and) the country of Ethiopia he had captured, and

11 ina la-mi-ni is-lu-la sal-la-aś-su
to a countless (extent) spoiled (carried off) its spoil;

12 MAT su-a-tu ina śi-khar-ti-sa i-bi-el-va
that country, through its whole extent, he ruled (over) and

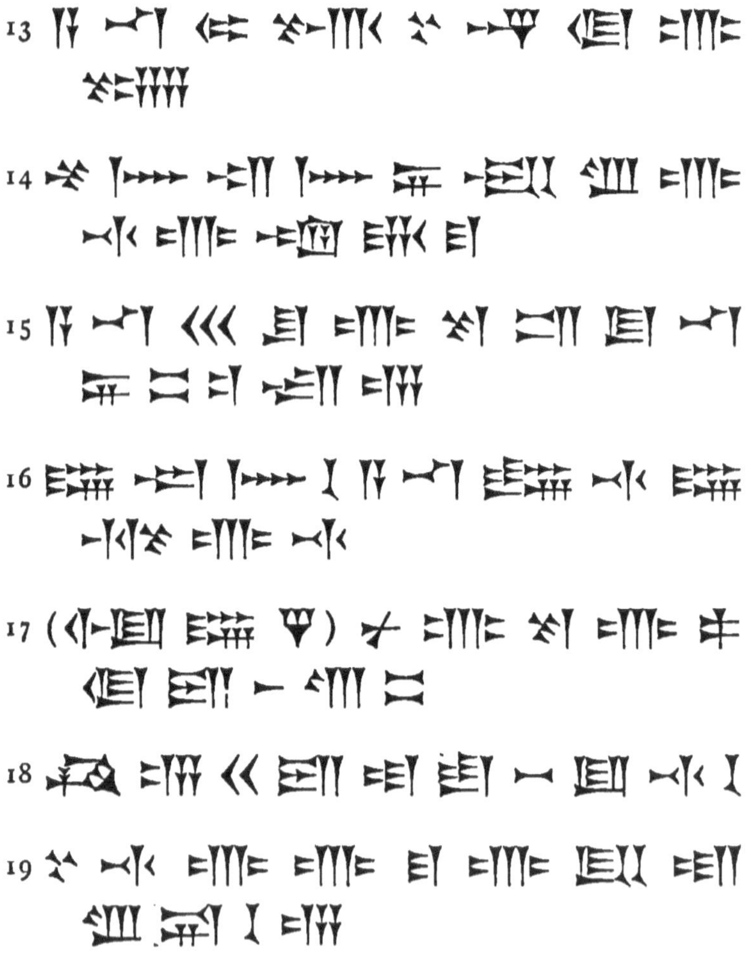
13
14
15
16
17
18
19

13 a-na mi-śir MAT ASSUR, D.A., yu-tir
for a border of the country of Assyria turned (it)

14 SUMI ALA-ni makh-ru-u-ti yu-nac-cir-va
the former names of the cities he made strange (abolished) and

15 a-na es-su-u-te is-cu-na ni-bi-iś-śu-un
afresh he established their names.

16 D.P., ARDI-su a-na SARRU-ti, D.P., PIKH-u-ti
His men-servants for kingships, prefects

17 va, D.P., sa-nu-u-te yu-pa-ki-da ina lib-bi
and governors he appointed within (it).

18 BILAT man-da-at-tu be-lu-ti-su
Offering (and) tribute to his lordship

19 sat-ti sam sam-ma yu-cin tsi-ru-us-su-un
yearly, a fixed sum he placed upon them.

K 3082. S 2027. K 3086.

OBVERSE.

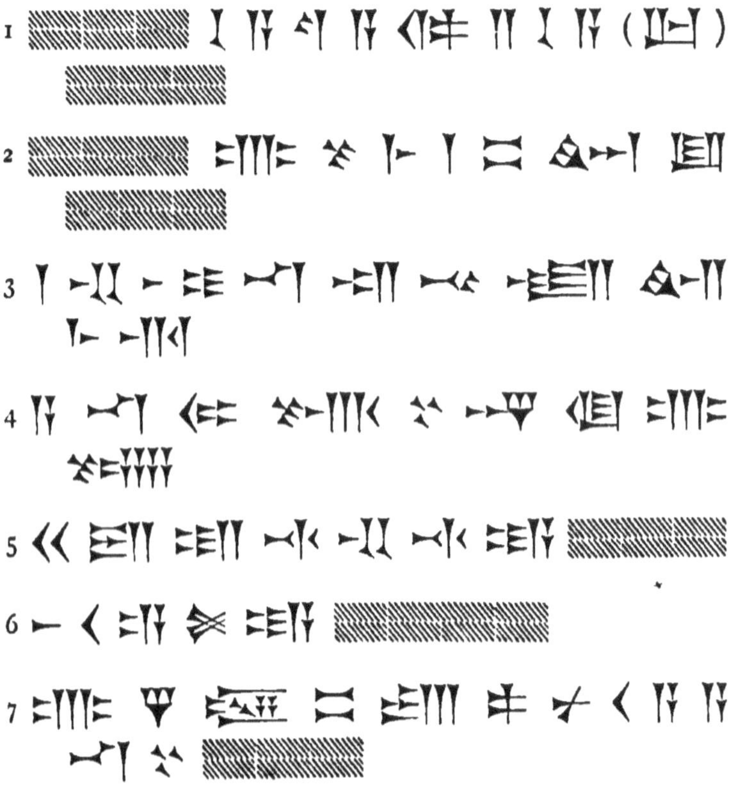

K 3082. S 2027. K 3086.

OBVERSE.

The tablet fragments (copies of which are printed below) were assigned by Mr. Smith to the reign of Esarhaddon, but there is nothing in them which proves it, and the style of writing appears to be more that of Assur-bani-pal than Esarhaddon.

Copies have been printed (*Trans. Soc. Bib. Arch.*, vol. iv. part 1, 1875), but the text there given is both incomplete and inaccurate; hence they are reprinted, and the text found on the tablet fragments is given.

1 . . . . . . su-a-tu a-di SANA ESSUTE a(lic) . . . . . .
(To) that (district) for the second time I went . . . . . .

2 . . . . . . u-se-sib, D.P., Bi-ah-lu . . . . . .
. . . . . . I caused to sit Biahlu (son of) . . . . . .

3 D.P., BEL-IDINNA i-na AL Kul-li-im-me-ri . . . . . .
Bel-idinna in the city of Kullimiri . . . . . .

4 a-na mi-śir MAT ASSUR, D.A., u-tir . . . . . .
to the border of the land of Assyria I brought back . . . . .

5 man-da-at-ti BIL-ti-ya . . . . . .
tribute to my lordship . . . . . .

6 Ina ESRIT-e KHARRAN-ya . . . . .
In my tenth expedition . . . . . .

7 u-sa-ats-bi-ta pa-nu-u-a a-na MAT . . . . .
I caused my face to take (the road) to the country of . . . .

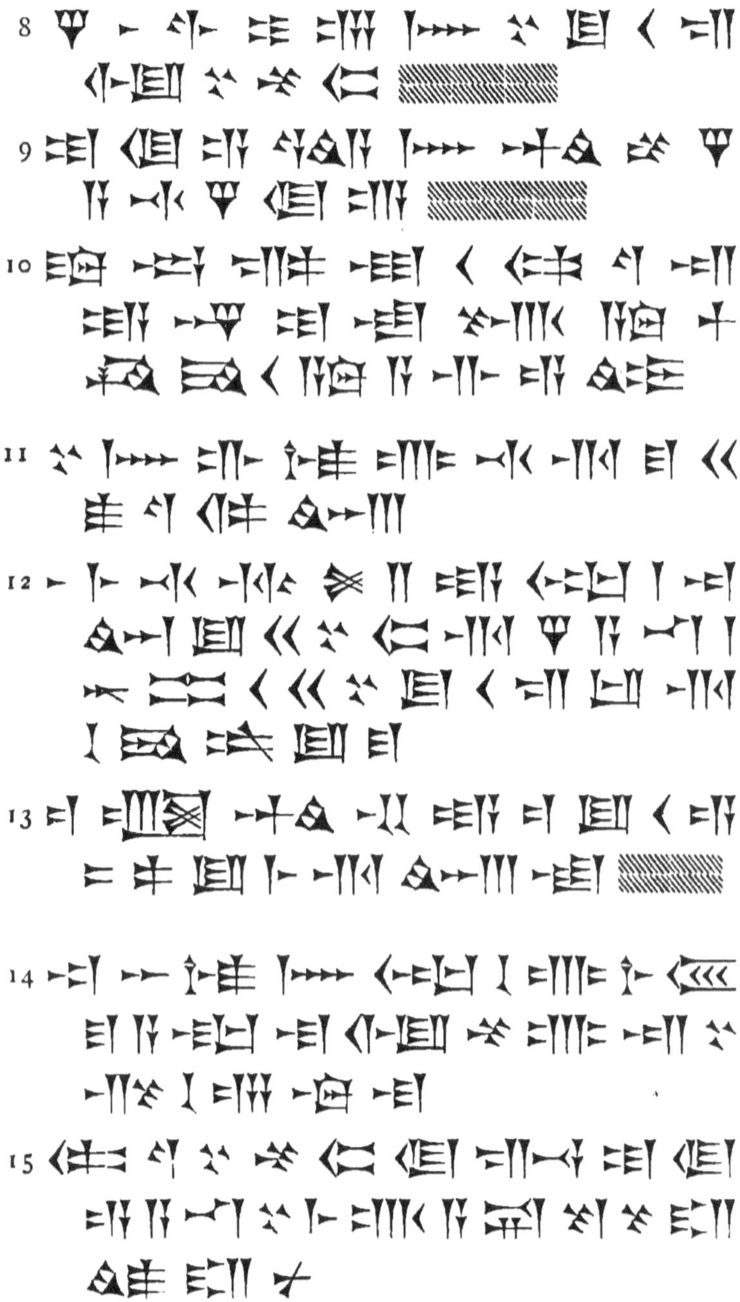

8 sa ina pi-i NISI MAT Cu-u-śi va MAT Mu-tsur . . . . . .
which (is called) in the language of the men of the land of Ethiopia and Egypt . . . . . .

9 ad-ci-e UMMANI, D.P., ASSUR gab-sa-a-ti sa ci-rib . . . . . .
I assembled the armies of Assur, mighty which (were) within . . . . . .

10 NISAN ARKHU ris-tu-u ul-tu AL-ya ASSUR at-tu-śir NAHR IDIKLAT U NAHR PUR-RAT (e-bir)
In the (month) Nisan, the first month, from my city Assur I departed, the river Tigris and the river Euphrates I crossed,

11 SADI mar-tsu-u-ti ri-ma-nis as-tam-di-ikh
mountains rugged, like a wild bull I passed through.

12 Ina me-ti-ik KHARRAN-ya eli, D.P., Ba-ah-lu SAR MAT Tsur-ri sa a-na, D.P., Tar-ku-u SAR MAT Cu-u-śi ip-ri-su it-tag-lu-va
In the crossing of my expedition against Bāhlu, king of Tyre, who to Tirhakah, king of the land of Ethiopia, his friend had trusted and

13 D.P., NIR, D.P., ASSUR BIL-ya iś-lu-u e-tap-pa-lu me-ri-ikh-tu . . . . . .
the yoke of the god Assur, my lord, they despised, they were insolent . . . ? . . .

14 D.P., khal-tsu(ti) eli-su u-rac-ciś va a-ca-lu va mu-u ba-ladh NAPIS-tiv-su-un ac-la . . . . . .
Fortresses against him I raised and food and water (for) the preservation of their lives I kept (from them).

15 ul-tu MAT Mu-tsur, D.P., CARASU ad-ci-e a-na MAT Me-lukh-a us-te-es-ra khar-ra-nu
From the country of Egypt the camp I withdrew and to the land of Melukha I set straight the road (expedition).

16 

17 

18 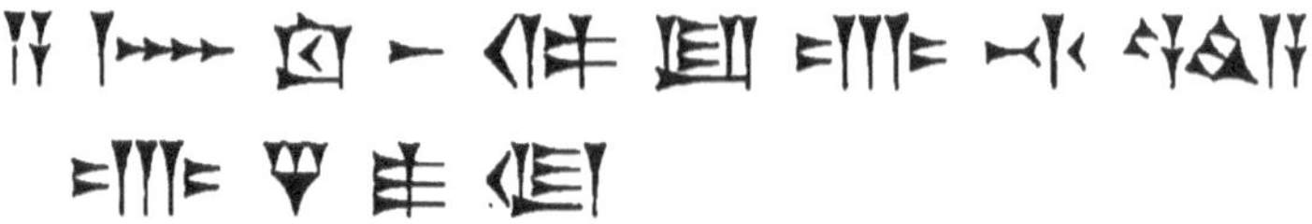

REVERSE.

1 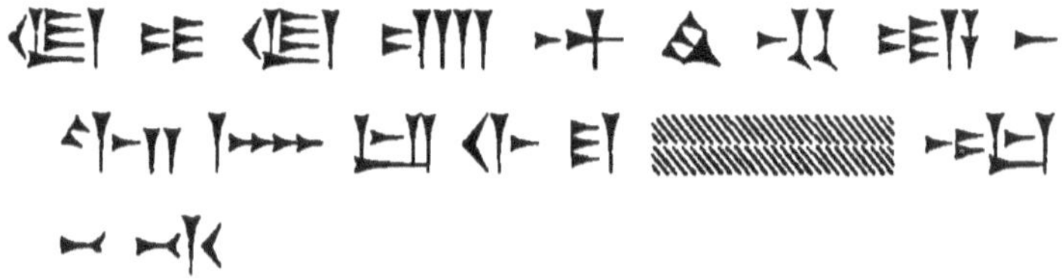

2 

3 

16 SILĀSA KAS-BU kak-kar ul-tu ALU Ap-ku sa pa-di MAT 'Sam-me-na . . . . . . a-di, D.P., Ra-pi-khi

Thirty *kasbu* of ground from the city Aphek, which borders the country of 'Samena . . . . . . to the city of Rapikhi,

17 a-na i-te-e na-khal MAT Mu-tsur a-śar NAHR la i-su-u ina ip-ri khar-khar-ri dan-dan-tu

to the frontiers of the valley of the country of Egypt, a region (which) a river had not, through dusty sunburnt places very great

18 MIE TSUTSI ina di-lu-u-ti UMMA-(ya) u-sa-as-ki

marsh waters from buckets, I caused my army to drink.

REVERSE.

1 ci-i ci-bit, D.P., ASSUR BIL-ya ina UZNA ip-si-va . . . . . . ca-bat-ti

When the command of the god Assur my lord, in my ears was also . . . . (then) my liver.

2 D.P., Gam-mal-li sa SAR MAT A-ri-bi ca-li-su-un . . . . . śu-nu-ti

Camels belonging to the king of Arabia, the whole of them . . . . . . them.

3 SILASĀ KASBU kak-kar ma-lac KHAMISSERIT YU-me ina . . . . . . ar-di . . . . . .

Thirty kasbu of ground, a journey of fifteen days in . . . . . . I marched . . . . . .

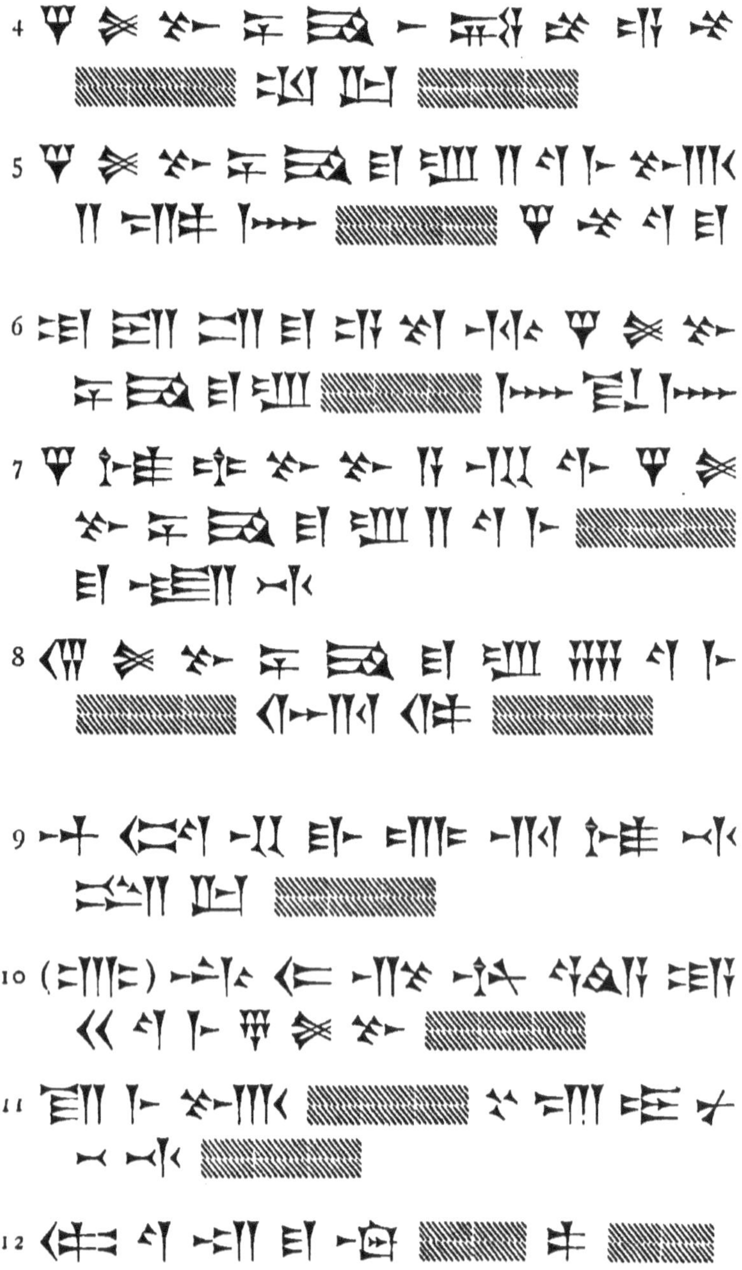

4 IV KAS-BU kak-kar ina, D.P., ... al-lic . . . . . .

Four kasbu of ground among . . . . . stones I went . . . . .

5 IV KASBU kak-kar ma-lac SANA YU-me TSIR SANA KAK-KADI . . . . . . sa mu-ut-va

Four kasbu of ground a journey of two days, snakes (with) two heads . . . . of death and

6 ad-da-is-va e-te-ik IV KAS-BU kak-kar ma-lac . . . . . BANI

I trampled upon and I passed through four kasbu of ground a journey . . . . . . gazelles

7 sa tsu-ub-bu-bu a-cap-pi IV KAS-BU kak-kar ma-lac SANA YU-me . . . . . . ma-li-ti

of lizards winged (?). Four kasbu of ground a journey of two days . . . . . . filled

8 KHAMISSERIT KAS-BU kak-kar ma-lac SAMNA YU-me . . . . . . ar-di

Fifteen kasbu of ground, a journey of eight days . . . . . . I marched.

9 D.P., MARDUK BIL RAB-u ri-tsu-ti il-lic . . . . . .

The god Merodach, the great lord (to my) help came . . . . . .

10 yu-pal-ladh NAPIS-tiv UMMAN-ya ESRĀ YU-me VII . . . . . .

he saved the life of my army. Twenty days, seven kasbu

11 sa me-śir . . . . . . MAT Mā-gan-nu bil-ti-ya . . . . . .

of the border . . . . . . of the land of Magannu (Sinai) my lordship . . . . . .

12 ul-tu, D.P., Ma-ak . . . . . . pa . . . . . .

from the city Maggan (?)

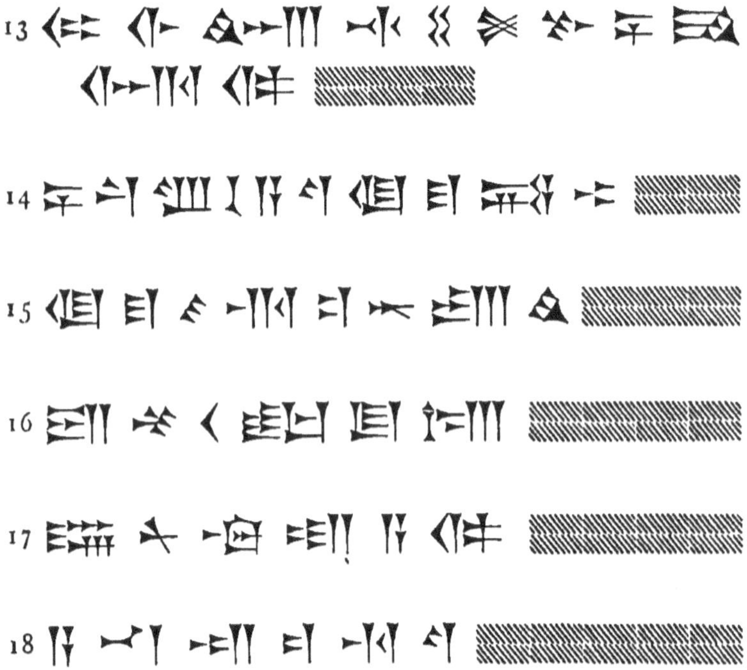
13
14
15
16
17
18

13 me-si-ikh-ti irbā KASBU kak-kar ar-di . . . . . .
a measurement of forty kasbu of ground, I marched . . . . .

14 kak-ka-ru su-a-tu ci-ma, D.P. . . . . . .
this ground like a . . . . . . stone . . . . . .

15 ci-ma tsip-ri, D.P., tar-ta-khi . . . . . .
like a heap of tartakhi . . . . . .

16 da-mu-u sar-cu el . . . . . .
(people of) blood white . . . . . .

17 D.P., NACIR ak-tsi a-di . . . . . .
a rebellious enemy to . . . . . .

18 a-na, D.P., Iś-khu-ut
To the city of Iśkhūt

LIST OF NAMES OF THE KINGS APPOINTED BY ESARHADDON TO RULE OVER DISTRICTS IN EGYPT.

(From the "Annals of Assur-bani-pal.")

W.A.I., iii. 17, 112.

112 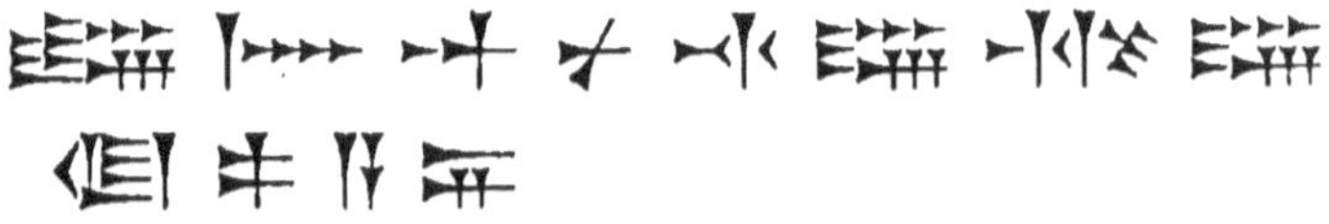

113 

W.A.I., iii. 17, 92–112.

92 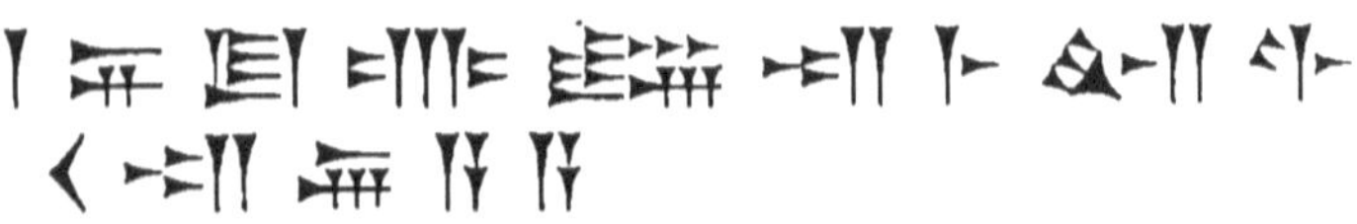

93 

94 

LIST OF NAMES OF THE KINGS APPOINTED BY ESARHADDON TO RULE OVER DISTRICTS IN EGYPT.

(From the "Annals of Assur-bani-pal.")

W.A.I., iii. 17, 112.

112 SARRANI an-nu-ti, D.P., PIKHATI, D.P., ci-pa-a-ni
These kings, prefects, (and) governors,

113 sa ci-rib MAT Mu-tsur u-pa-ki-du ABU ba-nu-u-a
which within the land of Egypt the father my begetter had appointed.

W.A.I., iii. 17, 92–112.

92 D.P., Ni-cu-u SAR, D.P., Me-im-pi u, D.P., S'a-ai
Necho King of Memphis and Sais

93 D.P., Sar-lu-da-ri SAR, D.P., Tsi-ah-nu
Sarludari, King of Tsihnu (Zoan ?)

94 D.P., Pi-sa-an-khu-ru SAR, D.P., Na-ad-khu-u
Pisan-Hor, King of Natho.

95 

96 

97 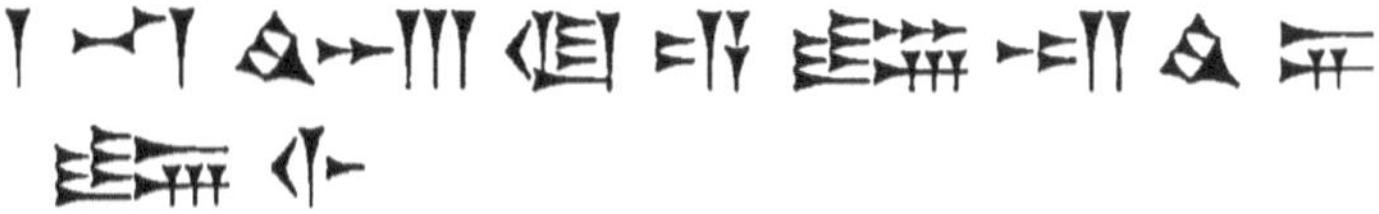

98 

99 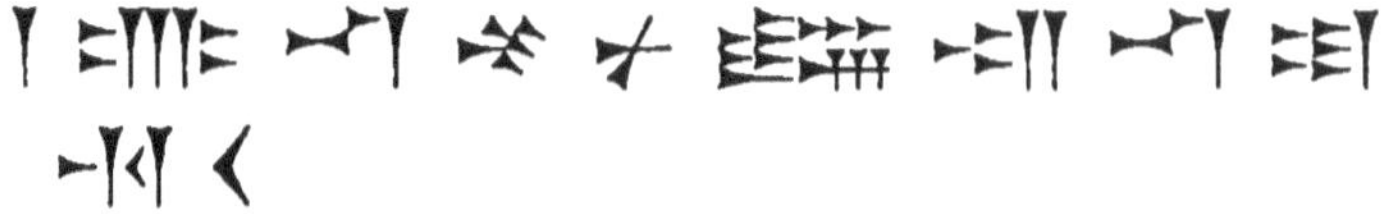

100 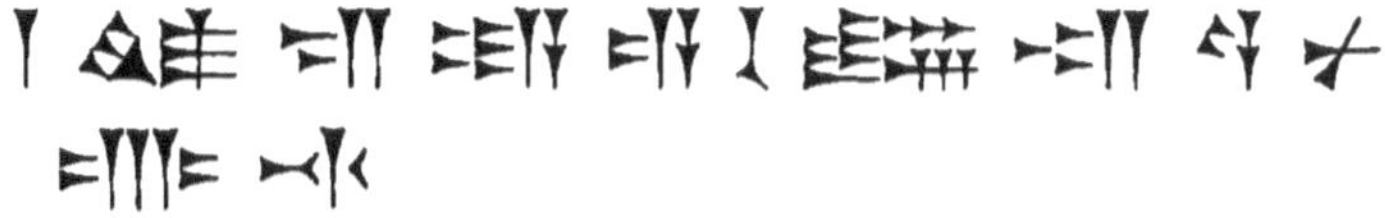

101 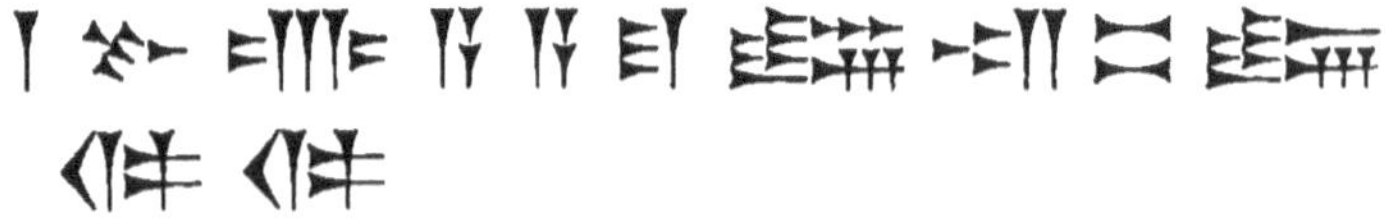

102 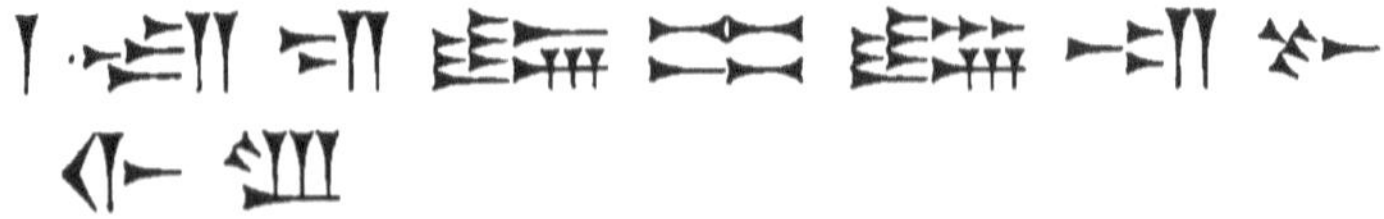

103 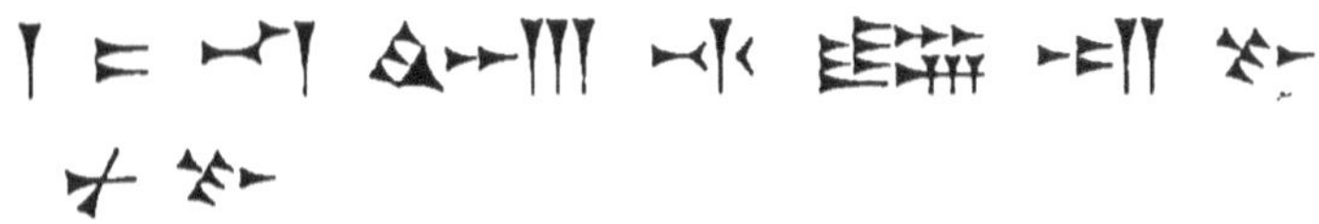

104 

95 D.P., Pa-ak-ru-ru SAR, D.P., (Pi) sab-tu
Pākruru, King of Pi-supt.

96 D.P., Pu-uc-cu-na-an-ah-pi SAR, D.P., Kha-at-khi-ri-bi
Puccunānahpi, King of Khātkhiribi.

97 D.P., Na-akh-ci-e SAR, D.P., Khi-ni-in-si
Nākhce, King of Khinīnsi (חנס).

98 D.P., Pu-dhu-bis-ti SAR, D.P., Tsa-ah-nu
Pudhubisti (Petubastes), King of Tanis (צען).

99 D.P., U-na-mu-nu SAR, D.P., Na-ad-khu-u
Unamunu, King of Nādkhū.

100 D.P., Khar-śi-ya-e-su SAR, D.P., Tsab-nu-u-ti
Kharśiyaesu, King of Tsabnūti (Sebennytus).

101 D.P., Bu-u-ai-va SAR, D.P., Bi-in-di-di
Būaiva, King of Bīndidi.

102 D.P., S'u-śi-in-ku SAR, D.P., Bu-si-ru
Sheshonk, King of Busiris.

103 D.P., Tab-na-akh-ti SAR, D.P., Bu-nu-bu
Tabnākhti, King of Bunubu.

104 D.P., Bu-uc-cu-na-an-ni-ah-pi SAR, D.P., Akh-ni
Būccunānniahpi, King of Akhni.

105 

106 

107 

108 

109 

110 

111 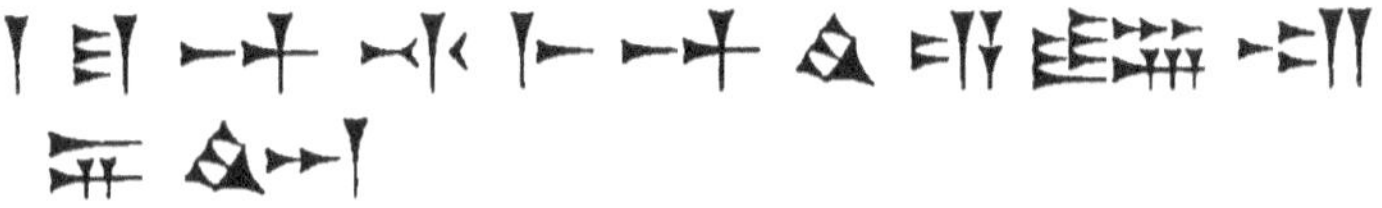

105 D.P., Ip-ti-khar-di-e-su SAR, D.P., Pi-za-at-ti-khu-ru-un pi-cu
Iptikhardiesu, King of Pizāttikhurūnpicu.

106 D.P., Na-akh-ti-khu-ru-an-śi-ni SAR, D.P., Pi-sab-di-nu-ti
Nākhtikhuruanśini, King of Pisabdinuti.

107 D.P., Bu-cur ni-ni-ip SAR, D.P., Pa-akh-nu-ti
Bucur-ninip, King of Pākhnuti.

108 D.P., Tsi-kha-a SAR, D.P., Si-ya-a-u-ut
Tsikhā, King of Siyāut.

109 D.P., La-me-in-tu SAR, D.P., Khi-mu-ni
Lamentu, King of Khimuni.

110 D.P., Is-pi-ma-a-dhu SAR, D.P., Ta-ai-ni
Ispimādhu, King of Tāini (Abydos).

111 D.P., Ma-an-ti-me-an-khi-e SAR, D.P., Ni-ah
Māntimeankhie, King of Thebes (נא).

VOCABULARY.

A

AB, fifth month of the Assyrian year. Explained by a syllabary . Heb. אָב. Its Accadian name is  , "fire that makes fire." (See *Trans. Soc. Bib. Arch.* iii. p. 163.)

A-AB-BA. The equivalent of the Semetic word "*tamate.*" (Layard's *Inscriptions*, plate 12, line 9.)

abbul, 1st sing. aor. Kal, for *anbul*. Heb. נָפַל.

abubu, subs. sing. masc., "storm," "whirlwind."

abulli, subs. sing. masc. gen. Chald. אֲבוּלָא, or אִיבוּלָא; this ideograph is explained *a-bul-luv*, K 4191, and *a-bu-ul-lu*, S 20.

Abdi-milcutti, *i.e.*, "the servant of the kingdom," or of Melkarth (?)

abduk, 1st sing. aor. Kal. Heb. דָּבַק, "to cleave."

abil, subs. sing. masc. cons. Comp. Heb. הֶבֶל (?).

abni, plu. masc. of *abnu*, 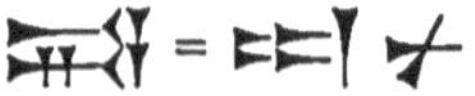 (iv. 18, 39). Heb. אֶבֶן.

abtani, 1st pers. sing. aor. Iphteal. Heb. בָּנָה.

abuca, 1st pers. sing. aor. Kal. Heb. אָבַךְ.

acalu, subs. fem. sing. Heb. אָכְלָה.

acappi, perhaps for *acanpi*. Comp. Heb. כָּנָף.

Accad. This is the Accad (אַכַּד) of Genesis x. 10. LXX. Ἀρχάδ. *Aca* is "high;" *acada*, "highlander;" *acada-ci*, "country of highlanders;" the *Accadai* descended from a mountainous country, but no part of Babylonia was mountainous.

N.B.—In the "Notes" references are made to the *Second* Edition of Prof. Sayce's *Grammar*. In such references as ii. 2, 393, the first number refers to one of the volumes of the *Cuneiform Inscriptions of Western Asia*, the second to the plate, and the third the line.

Among the Semetic Assyrians it bore the names of *tilla* and *saki*. *Tilla* = "highland" (ii. 48, 13). Heb. תְּלַל. SAKI = *summits* from Accad. SAK, "a head." SAK = risu (ii. 7, 36) Heb. רֹאשׁ. The inhabitants spoke an agglutinative dialect. Considerable discussion has existed between scholars as to whether the language should be called Sumerian or Accadian, and also where Accad was situated. On s 463 it is written , *Ac-cad-i* and *Ac-ca-di-iv* (i. 65, 9). The sign  is the D.A. for "country." (See Dr. Oppert, *Sumérien ou Accadian*, Paris, 1876; Prof. Sayce, *Assyrian Lectures*, p. 17; Dr. Delitzch, *Chaldäische Genesis*, p. 291 *et seq.*)

acbis, 1st sing. aor. Kal. Heb. כָּבַשׁ.

acin, 1st sing. aor. Kal. Heb. כּוּן.

acci, 1st sing. aor. Kal, for *anci*. Heb. נָכָה.

accisa for *ancisa*, 1st sing. masc. aor. Kal. Aram. נכס, "mactavit."

acla, 1st sing. obj. aor. Kal. Heb. כָּלָא.

acvu, 1st sing. aor. Kal. Heb. כָּוָה.

adi, prep. Heb. עַד.

addi, 1st sing. aor. Kal. Heb. נָדָה.

addin, 1st sing. aor. Kal. Heb. נָתַן.

aduc, 1st sing. aor. Kal. Heb. דָּכָה.

Adumu; Old Test. אֱדוֹם, Ἐδώμ; New Test. Ἰδουμαία. The country lay along the east side of the great valley of Arabah, and embraced only the narrow mountainous tract (about 100 miles long by 20 broad) extending along the eastern side of the Arabah, from the northern end of the gulf of Elath to near the southern end of the Dead Sea. Its ancient capital was *Bozrah* (Smith, *Bible Dict.*).

aggur, 1st sing. aor. Kal for *angur*. Heb. נָקַר.

agguri, subs. sing. masc. gen.

aiab, subs. sing. masc. cons. Heb. אוֹיֵב.

ai-ipparku, *ai*, negative particle. Comp. Heb. אִי, in Job xxii. 30, and 1 Sam. iv. 21; *ipparku*, Niph. aor., Heb. פָּרַק.

akartav, adj. plu. fem. Heb. יָקָר; comp. Collect אֶבֶן יְקָרָה, 1 Kings x. 2.

akhi, subs. masc. sing. gen. Heb. אָח.

akhi-enna, for *akh-anna*; *akh* = "a side," *anna* = demons. pron. sing. masc.

Akhi-milci. Comp. Heb. name אֲחִימֶלֶךְ.

akhai, "others," plu. Heb. אָח.

akhutav, abstract fem. Heb. אָח.

akrabi, subs. plu. masc. Heb. עַקְרַבִּים. (See GIR-TAB.)

akri, 1st sing. aor. Kal. Heb. קָרָא.

aktabi, 1st sing. aor. Iphteal. Chald. קְבַע.

aktasad, 1st sing. aor. Iphteal. Arab. *kashada.*

aktsu, adj. Heb. קָצָה, "to destroy."

AL, subs. sing. cons. of *alu*, "a city;" plu. *alani.* 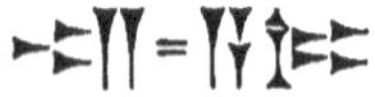 (ii. 2, 393). Heb. אֹהֶל.

alpi, subs. plu. masc of *alpu*. Heb. אֶלֶף.

alul, 1st sing. aor. Kal. Heb. עָלַל.

alve, 1st sing. aor. Kal. A verb doubly defective. Heb. לָוָה.

amas, 1st sing. aor. pres. Heb. מָשָׁה.

Amgurruna; Biblical עֶקְרוֹן; LXX. Ἀκκαρών.

amur, imperative, 2nd sing. Kal.

ana, prep., objective case of old noun *anu* (Sayce, *Grammar*, Trübner, page 142).

anacu, 1st pers. pron., sometimes written . Heb. אָנֹכִי.

ankhus'unu, for *ankhut-sunu*, subs. plu. masc. ענה.

anaru, 1st sing. perf. Kal. Heb. נִיר.

annadir, 1st sing. masc. aor. Niph. Comp. Heb. נָתַר, "to tremble."

anni. Comp. Heb. חָנַן.

annu, subs. sing. A synonym of *khidhitu.* Heb. עָוֹן.

Apku. The city Aphek. Comp. Heb. name אֲפֵק.

apsāni, subs. plu. masc. Sir H. Rawlinson thinks from *basu*, "to exist" (*Jour. R.A.S.*, xii. 190).

apta, 1st sing. aor. Kal. Heb. פָּתַח.

arbai, or *irbittu*, "four." Heb. אַרְבַּע.

arca, subs. sing. masc. Heb. יְרֵכָה.

arca, prep. Heb. אָרֵךְ.
ardi, subs. sing. masc. gen. Heb. רָדָה, "to rule over;" hence "one ruled over."
ardi, 1st sing. masc. aor. Kal. Heb. יָרַד.
ardu, see *ardi* above.
ARD-*uti*, subs. fem. abs. sing. Heb. רָדָה.
Aribi, 'Αραβία. The country known in the Old Test. under two designations—

(1) אֶרֶץ קֶדֶם, "the east country" (Gen. xxv. 6).
(2) עֲרָב, Arabia.

It was divided by the Greeks into—

(1) Arabia Felix (ἡ εὐδαίμων 'Αραβία).
(2) „ Deserta (ἡ ἔρημος 'Αραβία).
(3) „ Petraea (ἡ Πετραία 'Αραβία).

(Smith's *Bible Dict.*)

arsisuva, 1st sing. aor. Kal. Syr. רשׁי, with pers. pron. and enclitic conjunction.
artsip, 1st sing. aor. Kal. Heb. רָצַף, "to arrange stones."
Aruadi; Biblical אַרְוַד.
asar, subs. sing. masc. cons. of *asaru*. Heb. אֲתַר.
ascun, 1st sing. aor. Kal. Heb. שָׁכַן.
asibut, subs. masc. plu. cons. Heb. יוֹשֵׁב.
aslula, 1st sing. aor. Kal. Heb. שָׁלַל. (And see Sayce, *Assyrian Lectures*, p. 86–88.)
asmē, 1st sing. aor. Kal. Heb. שָׁמַע.
aspuc, 1st sing. aor. Kal. Heb. שָׁפַךְ.
AŚI,  =  , a synonym of *aricu*, "length," Heb. ארך; and  =  , *kar-nu*, "a horn," Heb. קֶרֶן (ii. 1, 176). Dr. Delitzch (*Ass. Stud.*, p. 35) thinks AŚI to be identical with  , "wild bull," and says it appears to be an animal with long horns.
asil, subs. sing. cons. Chald. אַשְׁלָא. The word used in the Targum on Job xviii. 10 to express the Heb. חבל.
asusur, 1st sing. aor. Shaph. Heb. אָשַׁר and יָשַׁר.
assi, 1st sing. masc. aor. Kal. Heb. נָשָׂא.

assu, prep. of Accadian origin (Sayce, *Grammar*, Trübner, p. 143).

as'sur, 1st sing. masc. aor. Niph. Heb. אָסַר, "to make captive."

Assur. The great and supreme god of the Assyrians, from which the country took its name. He is called the "god of judges" (iii. 66, 23), and the month Ve-adar was dedicated to "the god Assur, the father of the gods" (iv. 33, 48). Among the earlier kings, in their invocations he is simply mentioned as one among a number of gods, but in the time of Assurbanipal he is often mentioned alone and with attributes of power.

Assur, Biblical אַשּׁוּר. *Assur* is itself a Turanian compound from , "water," and  (*sur*), "bank or field," and has therefore attached to it the Accadian suffix , "land" (Sayce, *Trans. Soc. Bib. Arch.*, vol. i. 299). The earliest form found is , *a-usar* (i. 6; No. 1, 3), 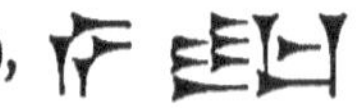 = *se-it-tu*, "field" (ii. 1, 145).

astadi, 1st sing. masc. aor. Iph. Heb. שׁוּד, "to lay waste."

atgul, 1st sing. masc. aor. Kal, from √ *dagalu*, "to trust."

atur, 1st sing. masc. aor. Kal.

atsbiru, 1st sing. perf. Kal. Heb. צָבַר.

atta, 2nd pers. pron. Heb. אַתָּה.

attabi, 1st sing. aor. Iph. Heb. נָבָא.

azcura, 1st sing. obj. aor. Kal. Heb. זָכַר.

Azdudi, Biblical אַשְׁדּוֹד, Ἄζωτός.

azkuppati, subs. plu. fem. Heb. זָקַף.

B

babani, subs. plu. Heb. בָּבָה.

baludh, subs. fem. cons. Comp. Heb. פְּלִיטָה.

bani. See *Assyrian Syllabary*, No. 313.

banū-a, or *banu-ya*, nom. agentis, masc. sing. Heb. בָּנָה.

baranu, comp. Heb. פָּרָא.

baru, a measure of length.

batli, subs. plu. masc.
Bāzu, probably the בּוּז of Jerem. xxv. 23; Gen. xxii. 21.
beli, subs. plu. masc. of *belu*. Heb. בַּעַל.
bilat, subs. fem. cons. Heb. בַּעֲלָה.
bilat, subs. fem. Heb. יָבַל, "to bring;"  = *bil-tu* (ii. 38, 14).
biluti, abstract fem. Heb. בָּעַל, "to rule over."
birmi, adj. plu. masc. Heb. בְּרוֹמִים (Ezek. xxvii. 24), "variegated garments."
biruti, adj. fem. Heb. בָּרָא, "to carve."
Bit-ammana. Mr. Smith compared the Biblical עַמּוֹן.
bitu, subs. sing. nom.  = *bi-i-tu* (ii. 2, 364). Heb. בַּיִת.
bussu, subs. masc., "spoil."
busūs, imperative Kal, from *basasu*.

C

cabatti, subs. fem. sing. Comp. Heb. כָּבֵד.
cabitti, subs. fem. sing. gen. (Same root.)
cabtu, adj. nom. (Same root.)
cacci, subs. plu. masc.
CA-DIMIRRA, the Biblical בָּבֶל. Its Accadian name was CA-DIMIRRA, D.A., meaning "the gate to god," of which the Semetic *bab-el* is an accurate translation.  =  , "gate" (ii. 2, 365). Heb. בָּבָה.

Its name is written in the following ways:—

 (i. 52, No. 6, 7).
 (i. 57, 28).
 (i. 18, No. 5).
 =  (i. 67, 16).

It bore the names of , DIN-TIR-CI (ii. 50, 2), properly the town on the western bank, and

 (i. 41, 16), SU-AN-NA-CI, properly the valley on the eastern bank. For the words "sons of Babylon" compare the Biblical usage "sons of Heth," "daughter of Zion."

calamu, "all the world," "of all kinds."

calata, permansive Kal, 2nd sing. masc. (with *ta* for *atta*). Heb. כָּלָא.

cali-sunu, adj., with 3rd plu. pers. pron. masc. Heb. כֹּל.

camīs, adv., from *camu*.

carani, subs. plu. Comp. קְרִינָא, "sweet wine."

carasi, subs. masc. gen., perhaps akin to Heb. רְכוּשׁ.

CASBU, CAS-BU = "double hour" in Accadian. Another form is , *kas-bu-mi*. The Assyrian equivalent is , *aṣ-li*. Chald. אַשְׁלָא, "a cord." The *casbu* was about 14 miles.

casid, subs. sing. cons. of nomen agentis. Arab. *kashada*.

cas'pu. The syllabaries render 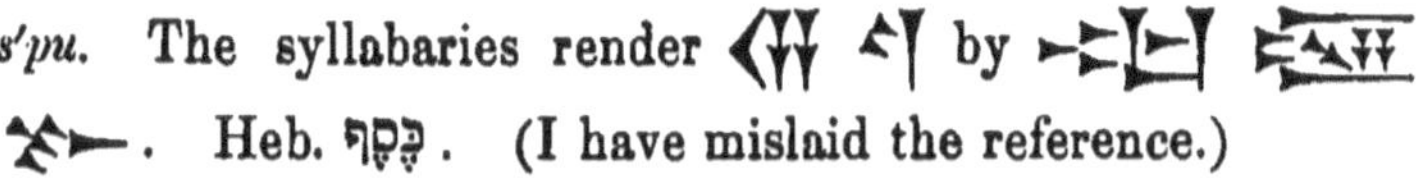. Heb. כֶּסֶף. (I have mislaid the reference.)

catrāi, subs. plu. masc. (See Norris, *Dict.*, p. 538.)

cavū, nom. agentis, masc. sing. cons. Heb. כָּוָה.

cazabiti. Comp. Heb. כָּזָב.

ci, prep. Heb. כִּי.

cibit, subs. fem. cons. with softened guttural. Heb. קְבַע.

cibitti, "abundance." Heb. כָּבֵד.

CILI = *ri-sa-a-tuv*, K 4357. Heb. רֹאשׁ.

cima, prep. Heb. כְּמוֹ.  (iv. 30, 5).

cinuv, adj. with mimmation. Heb. כּוּן.

cipāni, subs. plu. masc., "rulers." Comp. Heb. כָּפָה, "to subdue;" hence "subduers," "rulers."

ci-pī. Comp. Heb. כְּפִי. 1 Chron. xii. 23.

cips'i, subs. plu. masc. of *cips'u*. Heb. כָּבַס.

circti, abs. fem. plu. Heb. כָּרַע, "to bend the knee."

cirib, prep. Heb. קֶרֶב.

ciru, subs. masc. sing.  = *ci-ru* (iv. 18; iii. 36). Heb. כּוּר.

cisadi, subs. masc. plu. See *Syllabary*, No. 161. M. Lenormant (*Trans. Soc. Bib. Arch.*, vi. p. 188) compares the Ghez *chĕsādē.*

cis'alla, subs. masc. sing. Of Accad. origin.

cis's'ati, subs. plu. fem. Comp. Chald. כְּנִישָׁא or כְּנִישְׁתָּא.

Cis'u, Kissos, King of Salamis.

citnusu, 3rd plu. masc., perman. Iphteal, from כנש.

citu, adj. Comp. Chald. כִּתּוּנָא; Gr. χιτών.

CU, a sort of wood.

culul. Comp. Heb. כְּלָל.

culluv, adj. with mimmation. Heb. כֹּ.

CUS'S'U, subs. sing. masc. Heb. כִּסֵּא; Syr. כורסיא. The ideograph is explained by *cu-us'-s'u* (ii. 46, 52).

Cūs'i. Biblical כּוּשׁ, or Ethiopia.

cūtstsu, partic. Kal. A cognate form exists in Arabic (see Freytag, *Lex.*, vol. i. p. 40).

D

dabu, subs. masc. Heb. דּוֹב.

dādme-su, reduplicated derived form (peculiar to verbs פ״א and פ״ו). Heb. אָדָם; *su* = pers. pron. Heb. הוּא.

dais, sing. masc. cons. nom. agentis. Heb. דּוּשׁ.

DAL*ti*, subs. fem. sing. Heb. דֶּלֶת. The ideograph is explained by *da-al-tu* (ii. 15, 2).  = "wood," and  = pi-tu-u, "to open" (iv. 69, 46). Heb. פָּתַח; hence the whole means "the opening piece of wood."

damku, adj. See *Syllabary*, No. 333. The ideograph is explained by *da-mi-ik-tuv* (ii. 46, 53).

damū, subs. sing. masc. Heb. דָּם.

DAN, a kind of wood. It is called *gis kibir*, or "coffin wood." *Syl.* No. 7 s, and is there explained by *nappatsu*, perhaps a Niphal deriv. from *pitsu*, "white." Heb. בּוּץ.

danan, subs. sing. masc. cons. Of Accad. origin.

dandantu, reduplicated form. The form *dandanti* occurs on K 2802.

danas'su for *dannat-su*, subs. fem. sing.

daris, adv. from *daru*. Heb. דוֹר, "an age."

dhabu, ideograph explained by *dha-a-bu* (iv. 7, 6). Heb. טוֹב.

dharid, sing. masc. cons., nom. agentis. Heb. טָרַד, "to thrust."

dhem, subs. masc. sing. cons. Chald. טְעֵם (Dan. iii. 10).

dhib. Comp. Heb. טוֹב.

dikhi. Compared by Dr. Delitzsch with Heb. דחה.

diluti, subs. plu. masc. Heb. דְּלִי.

dur, subs. masc. sing. Heb. דוֹר, "a habitation."

E

ebir, 1st sing. aor. Kal. Heb. עָבַר.

edhil, 1st sing. aor. Kal. Heb. טלל, טול.

E-GAL. In Accad. = "great house." Heb. הֵיכָל. The ideograph is equated with *e-gal* (iv. 5, 31).

ekili, subs. plu. masc., and see ii. 70, 9, where  = Phœn. חקלא. Chald. חֲקַל. It is written *e-ki-il* (see *Jour. R.A.S.*, 1864, p. 209).

ellamūha, for *ellamū-ya*. Comp. Heb. עָלָה, "to go up;" hence "to be above," or "beyond."

ellat-s'u, subs. plu. masc. Heb. חַיִל, with *s'u* for *su*.

elamti. Biblical עֵילָם; Ἐλάμ; Aelam. The inhabitants were originally a Semetic people (Gen. x. 22) who appear to have been invaded and conquered at a very early time by a Hamatic or Cushite race from Babylon, called by the Greeks Κίσσιοι (Cissians). Its ancient capital was Susa. See Smith's *Babylonia* for its early history.

eli, prep. עַל.

emid, 1st sing. aor. Kal. Heb. עָמַד.

emū, 3rd plu. masc. aor. Kal. Comp. Heb. עָמַם.

emuki, subs. sing. masc. gen. Heb. עָמֹק.

ennu, subs. sing. nom. A synonym of *khidhita*, "sin" (*Chaldäische Genesis*, p. 306).

entenna, Iphteal deriv. Perhaps akin to עָנַן. According to Dr. Delitzsch it = Ass. *kutstsu*, "earthquake." Prof. Sayce thinks it an Accadian word.

enuva, adv. compounded of *enu*, and the pronoun *ma*, "that" (Sayce, *Grammar*, p. 115).

eparku, 3rd sing. masc. perf. Kal. Heb. פָּרַק.

eri, subs. masc. gen. Perhaps from Accad. *urudu*.

erib, subs. cons. Comp. Heb. עֶרֶב, "evening," from עָרַב, "to set like the sun."

erinu, subs. sing. masc. Heb. אֹרֶן. Written also *e-ri-ni* and *ir-ni*.

eris'ina = *erid-sina*. Comp. Heb. רָדָה.

erisu, 3rd plu. masc. aor. Kal.

esci, subs. sing. masc. (But text very doubtful.)

esrā. Comp. Heb. עֶשְׂרִים.

esrit, ord. number. Heb. עֶשְׂרֵה.

esru, fem. card. number. Heb. עֶשֶׂר.

essute, for *edsute*. Comp. Heb. חָדַשׁ, "to be new."

ESTEN, an Accadian word compounded of , *as*, "one," and , *ta-a-an* (ii. 10, 21), "a measure," lit. "one measure." It is the word from which the Heb. עַשְׁתֵּי in the number "eleven" is derived. See Dr. Oppert, *Grammaire Assyr.*, pp. 32–38, second edition.

etappalu, 3rd plu. masc. aor. Pael. Heb. עָפַל. Comp. וַיַּעְפִּילוּ, "they acted insolently" (Num. xiv. 44).

etek, 1st sing. aor. Kal. Heb. עָתַק.

eteittik, 1st sing. masc. aor. Ittaphal. Heb. עָתַק.

G

gabal, subs. sing. masc. cons. Heb. גְּבִילָה.

gabsuti, "strong," adj. fem.

GAL = *rabu*, "great." Heb. רַבָּה.

gammali, subs. plu. masc. Heb. גָּמָל.

GIDDA = *a-ric*, "length" (ii. 46, 7). Heb. אָרַךְ.

gigu, subs. sing. masc. Heb. גַּג.

gimir, cons. of *gimiru*. Heb. גָּמַר, "to be complete."

Gimirrai. The גֹּמֶר of Gen. x. 2; probably the CIMMERII (Κιμμέριοι), remarkable for their incursions into Asia Minor in the 6th century B.C. (Herod. i. 6, 15, 103; iv. 1, 11, 12). They took Sardis B.C. 635 (Smith's *Class. Dict.*, art. "Cim.")

girri, subs. plu. masc. Heb. גָּרָה, "to make war."

GIR-TAB, see under *akrabi*. Concerning winged snakes or scorpions, see Rawlinson's *Herod.* ii. p. 499.

Gūbli, Biblical גְּבַל.

gusuri, subs. plu. masc. The ideograph is explained by *gu-su-ra* (ii. 15, 12).

H

halic, 2nd sing. masc. imperative, Kal. Heb. הָלַךְ.

I

ibbu, adj. Heb. יָפָה.

ibel, 3rd sing. masc. aor. Kal. Heb. בָּעַל.

icbus'u, 3rd plu. masc. aor. Kal. Heb. כָּבַשׁ.

icnusu, 3rd plu. masc. aor. Kal, √ כנשׁ.

icsudu, 3rd sing. masc. perf.

idā-ca, subs. dual. Heb. יָד; *ca* = ךָ.

idcie, 3rd sing. masc. aor. Kal.

idū, 1st sing. aor. Kal. Heb. יָדַע.

idiclat. The river Tigris. In line 35 of the Behistun inscription it is written *di-ik-lat*, which Mr. Norris compared to the Hiddikel (חִדֶּקֶל) of Genesis ii. 14. Called by the Arameans דִּגְלָא. Syr. דקלת. *idiclat* is the Semetic equivalent of A-SUS-MAS-TIG-GAR. It is sometimes written ►► ►►.

igug, 3rd sing. masc. aor. Kal. M. Guyard (in *Journal Asiatique*, Jan. 1880) makes this come from √ *nagagu*, "to cry," "to groan;" M. Halévy from √ *agagu*, "to be angry;" and see iv. 2, 37.

ikribi, subs. plu. masc. Heb. קָרַב, "to approach."

iksuda, 3rd sing. masc. obj. aor. Kal.

iksudu, 3rd sing. masc. perf. Kal.

iktarrabu, 3rd plu. masc. aor. Iph. Heb. קָרַב.

ilabbiru, 3rd sing. masc. fut. Kal, from √ *labaru*, "to be old."

ilbinu, 3rd plu. masc. aor. Kal. Heb. לָבֵן, denom. לְבֵנָה.

ili and *ilani*; plu. of *ilu*, "god." Heb. אֵל. The plural is once written  (Heb. אֱלֹהִים), *i-lim* (preserving the mimmation) in the name of *Assur-ris-ilim*—*i.e.*, "Assur, chief of the gods" (i. 6, No. 5, 2).

illicavva, 3rd sing. obj. aor. Kal. Heb. הָלַךְ, with mimmation and enclitic *va*.

ilubusu, 3rd sing. masc. perf. Kal. Heb. לָבַשׁ.

ilve, 3rd sing. masc. aor. Kal. Heb. לָוָה.

imguru, 3rd plu. masc. aor. Kal.

imiri, subs. plu. masc. Heb. חֲמוֹר. The initial ח being lost, as in the word *ekil*, "land" (which see).

imkhatzu, 3rd sing. masc. perf. Kal. Heb. מָחַץ.

imnu. Heb. יָמִין. This sign (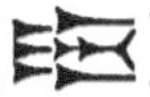) happens to mean "left hand," as well as .

ina, prep., obj. case of the old noun *inu*, being identical with Heb. יַעַן (Sayce, *Gram.*, Trübner, p. 142).

inakhu, 3rd sing. masc. fut. Kal. √ ענה.

inambū, 3rd plu. masc. pres. Kal. Heb. נָבָא.

inaru, 3rd plu. masc. Comp. Heb. נִיר.

indalīkhkhu, 3rd sing. masc. perf. Niph. Heb. דָּלַח, "to trouble."

innabtu, 3rd sing. masc. perf. Niph.

in-summa, "in all," "altogether."

ipri, subs. sing. masc. Heb. חָבֵר.

ipri, adj. masc. Heb. עָפָר.

ipsi, 3rd sing. masc. aor. Kal, from √ *basu*, "to be."

ipsit, fem. abstract sing., from √ *episu.*

ippalcitunivva, 3rd sing. masc. perf. Niph., with enclitic *va.*

ipparsidu, 3rd sing. masc. perf. Niph. Heb. פָּרַשׁ, "to spread out."

irbā. Comp. Heb. אַרְבָּעִים.

irdu, 3rd sing. masc. perf. Kal. Heb. יָרַד.

iritsi, subs. sing. gen.

irsi, 3rd sing. masc. aor. Kal. √ רשי.

irti, "against," of doubtful origin.

irtsitiv, subs. fem. sing. Heb. אֶרֶץ.  = *ir-tsi-tiv* (ii. 1, 182).

isadha, 3rd sing. telic. obj. aor. Kal. √ שום.

isal, 3rd sing. masc. pres. Kal. Heb. שָׁאַל.

isati, subs. fem. sing. Heb. אִשׁ; Eth. *ěsât*; Chald. אִשָּׁא. The word is once found written phonetically  (3 Mich. i. 34). It is remarkable that it only wants the sign  to complete the name of the solar hero Gisdhubar .

iscuna, 3rd sing. masc. obj. aor. Kal. Heb. שָׁכַן.

iscunu, 3rd sing. masc. perf. Kal. (Same root.)

isimmu, 3rd plu. masc. fut. Kal. Heb. שָׁמַע.

Iskaluna. Biblical אַשְׁקְלוֹן; 'Ασκάλων.

is'khappu, subs. masc. sing. Heb. סָחַף.

is'lu, 3rd plu. perf. Kal. Heb. סָלָה.

islula, 3rd sing. masc. obj. aor. Kal. Heb. שָׁלַל.

isme, 3rd sing. masc. aor. Kal. Heb. שָׁמַע.

ispuravva, 3rd sing. masc. obj. aor. Kal, and enclitic *va.* Arab. *sapara.*

isruca, 3rd sing. masc. obj. Kal. Heb. שָׂרַךְ.

istapparunivva, 3rd sing. masc. perf. Iph. with enclitic *va.*

Istar. The Biblical עַשְׁתֹּרֶת; Greek 'Αστάρτη. A goddess, "the lady of war and battle," who played a great part in the religious system of the Assyrians. Istar was the daughter of the Moon-god, her spouse was Tammuz (the תַּמּוּז of Ezekiel viii. 14), and the Adonis of the Greeks, whom she went to seek in the "land of no return," or Hades. Many are the hymns which are dedicated to Istar, and very fine are the epithets applied to her. As her name is written here, she is the goddess of the half-month, or fifteen days (). She is called "the wife of Bel" (iii. 24, 78). As regards the title "Istar of Nineveh," it is said (iii. 24, 65): *Istar sa Ninua il-sarrat Kitmure*, "Istar of Nineveh, the divine queen of Kitmure;" and in line 78 Nineveh is said to be *naram Istar*, "the delight of Istar." The month Elul was dedicated to her. There were also Istar of Arbela, and Istar of Erech. (See the remarks and authors quoted in Gesenius, *Thesaurus*, p. 1082.)

issikta, for *insikta*. Comp. Heb. נָשַׁק.

is's'uni, 3rd plu. masc. perf. Kal. Heb. נָשָׂא; as in 1 Kings x. 12.

izcuru, 3rd plu. masc. aor. Kal. Heb. זָכַר.

ita, subs. fem. sing.

itbalu, 3rd sing. masc. perf. Iphteal. Heb. יָבַל.

itēru, 3rd plu. masc. aor. Kal. Heb. תּוּר.

iteti, subs. plu. fem., "frontiers."

itstsarīkh, 3rd sing. masc. aor. Niph. = *ikabbi* (iv. 11, 30). Chald. קְבַע.

itstsuri, subs. masc. sing. Heb. צִפּוֹר.

itibbu, 3rd sing. masc. perf. Iphteal. Heb. בָּנָא.

itta, "a military ensign." Heb. אוֹת (see Numb. ii. 2).

ittagil, 3rd sing. masc. pres. Niph., from √ *dagalu*. A verb peculiar to Assyrian.

ittallacu, 3rd pers. sing. masc. perf. Iphteal. Heb. הָלַךְ, with *va* enclitic like Latin "que."

itti, prep. Heb. אֵת.

K

kabal, subs. sing. cons. Comp. Heb. קֳבַל.

kakkadi, subs. plu. masc. Heb. קָדְקֹד.

kakkar, subs. masc. sing. cons. Heb. כִּכָּר, "a tract of country" (Neh. xii. 28).

kakkas'u, for *kakkad-su*, for *kad-kad-su* (see *kakkadi*).

kaldi. The land of Caldu or Kaldu is first mentioned by Assur-natsir-pal (i. 24, 1), B.C. 878, and in the year B.C. 850, his son Shalmaneser speaks of the district as lying below Babylonia, on the Persian Gulf. The word *casdim* is best explained by the Assyrian root *casadu*, "to conquer," "to possess" (Sayce, *Lectures*, pp. 49 and 61).

kan. Comp. Heb. קָנֶה,  (ii. 24, 6).

karan, subs. masc. sing. cons. Heb. קֶרֶן.

kasbu, see *casbu*.

katai, subs. dual masc. with pron. suff. Comp. Targum קַתָּא, "a handle."

katav, subs. plu. (Same root.)

khabbilu, Pael, adj. Heb. חָבַל, "to destroy."

khaltsuti, subs. plu. Comp. Heb. חָלַץ (No. 2).

khamisserit. Comp. Heb. חֲמִשָּׁה עָשָׂר.

khamsa, fem. card. number. Heb. חֲמִשָּׁה.

kharkharri, subs. plu. masc. Comp. Heb. חֲרֵרִים, "sunburnt places" (Jerem. xvii. 6).

kharran, subs. sing. cons. Of Accadian origin. Its synonyms are *daragu*, Chald. דַּרְגָּא; and *metiku*, from √ *etiku*, Heb. עָתַק (see ii. 52, 3).

kharru, subs. masc. sing. Heb. חוּר.

kharsani, subs. masc. plu. of *kharsu*. Heb. חֹרֶשׁ.

khatti. The Biblical חֵת (Gen. xxiii. 3).

khattu, subs. fem. sing.

khaziti. Biblical עַזָּה; Γάζα.

khidhdhu, subs. fem., of Pael formation. Heb. חֵטְא.

khilacci. The classical CILICIA in S.E. of Asia Minor.
khisakhti, subs. plu. fem. Chald. חֲשַׁח.
khubūt, subs. fem. cons. plu., "booty," √ חבט.
khūd, subs. cons. Heb. חָדָה, "to be glad."
khuratsu. The ideograph is explained by *khu-ra-tsu* (ii. 1, 111). Heb. חָרוּץ.
kullultav, subs. plu. fem. Heb. קְלָלָה.
kuradi, subs. plu. masc.
kutu = *Gutium* (Kurdistan), the גּוֹיִם of Gen. xiv.

L

lābbis, adv. from *labbu.* Heb. לֵב.
labini, subs. plu. masc. Heb. לְבֵנִים.
la-isā. Comp. Syr. לית.
la-isū, 3rd pers. sing. masc. perf. Kal. Heb. יָשָׁה, with negative *la.* Heb. לֹא.
lalā, from Accad. *lal*, "to fill."
lapān, prep. Heb. לִפְנֵי.
la-s'āngu, a synonym of *la-ma-gi-ru* (ii. 27, 41), "disobedient."
libbi, subs. masc. sing. gen. Heb. לֵב.
Libnana. The Biblical לְבָנוֹן.
LICCU =  *cal-bu* (ii. 6, 13). Heb. כֶּלֶב.
limneti, subs. plu. fem., perhaps Heb. לָחַם, "to fight."
limni, subs. plu. masc. (Same root.)
listaprū, 3rd plu. masc. prec. Iphteal.
liti, subs. plu. fem.
liveti. Comp. Heb. לָוָה, "to be around."
lubulti, for *lubusti*, *s* changing into *l* before a dental, subs. fem. sing. Heb. לְבוּשׁ.
lūddis, 3rd sing. masc. prec. Aphel. Comp. Heb. חָדַשׁ, in Piel to repair buildings (1 Sam. xi. 14).

lulie. From Accadian.
lūsbā, 3rd. sing. prec. Kal. Heb. שָׂבַע.
lutassib, 2nd sing. masc. prec. Pael. Heb. יָשַׁב.

M

Madai. Inhabitants of the Biblical מָדַי. They occupied the country, called after their name, which lies to the N.W. of Persia proper. They were descendants of Japhet.
madātte, for *maudante,* subs. fem., lit. "something given." Comp. מַתְּנָן, Dan. ii. 6.
Magannu. "The ship region." And see Lenormant, *Les Noms de l'Airain,* etc. (*Trans. Soc. Bib. Arch.,* vi. p. 350).
Māhba. Biblical מוֹאָב.
māhdis, adv. from *mahdu.* Heb. מְאֹד.
makhazi, for *makhatsi,* subs. plu. masc. Heb. מַחַץ.
makhkhi, adj. from Accad. MAKH.
makhira, subs. sing. masc. accus. case of *makhar,* √ מחר.
makhriti, prep. fem. form.
makhrute. "Previous, former."
malū, 3rd. plu. masc. perf. Kal. מָלֵא.
māllu, partic. Kal. (Same root.)
mamit, subs. fem. sing. Heb. אֲמָנָה.
mana, subs. masc. plu. Heb. מָנֶה, Gr. μνᾶ. The standard maneh appears to have been fixed at Carchemish. There seem to have been manehs of different weight and value; thus:—

5 manehs of silver = 2 manehs of gold.
10 " " = 1 " "

(*Records of the Past,* i. p. 166.)

Mannai. The Biblical מִנִּי, of Jer. li. 27. Proper name of a province which is joined with אֲרָרָט according to Bochart; Μινυάς, "a tract of Armenia" (Gesenius), placed by Rawlinson (Herod i. 464) about Lake Urumiyeh, and with the Minuas who appears in the list of ancient kings in the inscriptions at Vau (Layard, *Nineveh and Babylon,* p. 401).

marab. Deriv. from *rabu*. Comp. Heb. מָרַב.

Marduk. The Biblical מְרֹדָךְ of Jer. l. 2. The name is Accadian, and means "the splendour (or light) of the sun."  *bu-ru*. Heb. בָּהַר (ii. 1, 156), and *tsūru*. Heb. צָהַר,  = *sam-su* (ii. 3, 431), "the sun." He was called *Silik-mulu-khi*, "the protector of the city who benefits mankind," and was the son of Hea () iv. 7, 25 (Sayce). The month Marchesvan was dedicated to "the Lord, the prince of the gods, Merodach" (iv. 33, 43). The name Marduk has been found written  , D.P., Ma-ru-duk (*Zeitschrift für Aeg Sprache*, July, 1869, p. 95), and  (see Norris, *Dict.*, p. 940).

Marduk-abla-idinna, "Marduk gave a son." Heb. מְרֹאדַךְ־בַּלְאֲדָן. His name is written  (Botta, 151).

martsis, adv. from *martsu*. Arab. *maritsa*, "to be wearied out with toil."

martsuti, adj. fem.

masac, subs. sing. masc. cons. of *masacu*. Syr. משכא.

mascit, subs. fem. sing. Heb. מָשַׁךְ, "to hold."

mascani, subs. sing. masc. gen. Heb. מִשְׁכָּן.

massate, adj. fem. Perhaps from √ משח, as compared by Mr. Norris.

mat. This sign is explained by *ma-a-tu* (ii. 39, 4). The Accadian name for land was *mada*, and this word is perhaps the original of the Aram. מתא. The following extract from Syl. 116, is interesting:—

Melukha. A word often used instead of Cush.
Menas'ic. The מְנַשֶּׁה of the Bible.
mesikhti, subs. fem. Heb. מָשַׁח.
mêsir, subs. masc. sing. cons. Heb. אָסַר.
metik, synonym of *kharran*, which see.
mie, subs. plu. masc. Heb. מַיִם.
milac, sub. masc. sing. cons. Comp. Heb. מַהֲלָךְ.
mimma, pron. Comp. Heb. מְאוּמָה.
mis'ir, see *mes'ir*.
mitpani, subs. sing. masc. A synonym of *Ka-as-tav* (ii. 19, 7, 8). Heb. קֶשֶׁת, √ תפן.
mitgari, adj., Iphteal deriv. √ *magaru*, "to be happy."
mu. Comp. Heb. מִי, Chald. מוֹי.
muahdie, adj. Heb. מְאֹד.
mukhadu, partic. Comp. Heb. חָדָה.
mukhkha. Assyrianized form of Accad. MUKH, "upon."
mukki. Of Accad. origin. (See ii. 1, 161.)
multauti, fem. abs. Comp. Heb. שָׁאָה, "to make a noise."
muni, subs. fem. sing. √ מְאַן. .
muppārsi, Niph. partic. Heb. פָּרַשׁ.
murnisci, subs. plu. masc. This word is by general consent translated war-horses.
musab, sub. sing. cons. Heb. מוֹשָׁב.
musallimu, Pael partic. nom. Heb. שָׁלַם.
musappīkh, Pael partic. masc. sing cons.
musare, subs. plu., like *nadie*, "gifts."
musaru, subs. sing. masc. Heb. יָשַׁר, "to be straight."
musezibi, partic. Shaph. Heb. עָזַב.
mussiccu, subs. sing. masc. nom. Heb. נָשַׁךְ.
mūt, subs. sing. cons. Chald. מוֹת.
mutsa, subs. sing. masc. Heb. מוֹצָא.
Mutsri. The Biblical מָצוֹר.

N.

nabali, subs. masc. sing. gen. case, Niph. form. Comp. Heb. בְהָלָה.

nabiah, subs. sing. masc. cons.

nabniti, subs. fem. Niph deriv. Heb. בָּנָה.

Nabu, "the prophet." Heb. נָבִיא. The god who was supposed to preside over literature. As befitted the god whose name meant a prophet, his consort's name was  , D.P., *Tas-me-tur*, "the hearer" (iv. 55, 26). He is the Biblical נְבוֹ. The 4th, 9th and 17th days of the month were days upon which the King sacrificed to Nebo (iv. 32, 17; 42, 31).

Nabu-sallim, "Nebo completes."

Nabu-zir-napisti-esir. "Nebo the seed of life (guides) straight."  = *asaru* and *isaru*. Heb. יָשַׁר.

Naci, 2nd sing. imp. Kal. Heb. נָכָה, "to kill," as in Gen. iv. 15.

naciru, subs. masc. sing. Heb. נֶכֶר.

naclis, adv. from *naclu*. Heb. כָּלָה.

nacmu, partic. Heb. כָּוָה. Niph. deriv.

nadan, subs. masc. sing. Heb. נָתַן. Talmud נדוניא.

nadic, subs. plu. masc. Heb. נָדָה.

nādu, adj.

nagū, subs. masc. sing., of Accad. origin  =  (ii. 1, 147).

Nahid-Merodach, "the majesty of Merodach." *Nahid*, a Niph. deriv.

nahr, subs. sing. masc. cons. Heb. נָהָר. The ideograph  means "flowing water." It is thought to have been pronounced HID in Accadian.

nakhal, subs. sing. masc. cons. Heb. נַחַל.

namcur, subs. masc., Niph. deriv. of *macaru*. Comp. Heb. מֶכֶר.

namri. adj. √ נמר, bright, clear.

napalcattanu, subs. masc. sing. Niph. collective in *anu*.

naparka. Niph. deriv. partic. Heb. מֶרֶק.

napsat-s'u, for *napsat-su*, subs. fem. sing. Heb. נֶפֶשׁ, with enclitic pron.

natsiru, 3rd plu. masc. permans. Kal. Heb. נָצַר.

niba, Pael partic. Heb. נָבָא, "to speak."

nibikhu. Comp. *nibkhu*, "the zenith." (See *nipikhu*.)

nibis's'un, for *nibit-s'un*, for *nibit-sun*, subs. plur. (See *niba*.)

nibit-s'u, for *nibit-su*, subs. fem. sing.

nināra, 1st plu. masc. pres. Kal. Heb. נָאַר.

ninguti, subs. plu. fem. Comp. Heb. נְגִינוֹת.

NIN-SUM-SU. See *Chaldäische Genesis*, p. 296.

Ninua. Biblical נִינְוֵה. Νινευι, Luke xi. 32. Literally it means the "fish city," for  = 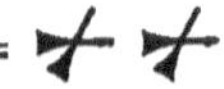 (ii. 7, 25); Heb. נוּן, "a fish." A city situated upon the banks of the Tigris, and the capital of Assyria. Its ancient name was  , NI-NĀ-A-CI (K 4629), and means "the resting-place of the god" (Delitzsch). Ninua was the daughter of Hea (iv. 1).

nipis'a, subs. sing. Heb. נֶפֶס.

nipikhu. This word occurs in Layard's *Inscriptions*, pl. xxxix. line 33. It is equated with *saruru* and *sabubu* (ii. 35, 8).

niri, subs. sing. masc. Heb. מָנוֹר. The ideograph is explained by *ni-i-ru* (ii. 4, 658).

Nisan. The first month of the Assyrian year. Assyr.  (Heb. נִיסָן); Accad.  , "the month of righteous (sacrifices)." It was dedicated to Anu and Bel. (See *Trans. Soc. Bib. Arch.*, iii. p. 162).

nisi, subs. plu. masc. Comp. Syr. אנשין.

nitsirti, subs. fem. sing. Lit. "the guarded things." Comp. אוֹצָרוֹת, "treasures" (2 Chron. xi. 11).
nittallac, 1st plu. masc. pres. Kal. Heb. הָלַךְ.
nītu. (Root uncertain.)
nūmmur, subs. cons. √ נמר.
nuni, subs. sing. masc. Heb. נוּן.
nupār-sun, subs. sing. with 3rd pers. pron. affix.

P

padi, subs. plu. masc. Comp. Heb. פֵּאָה. Chald. פָּאתָא for *pati*, like *tamdi*, for *tamti*.
pagar, subs. sing. cons. Heb. פֶּגֶר. The sense here requires the plural.
pakadi, subs. masc. gen. case. פָּקַד.
pakidat, subs. fem. sing. cons. (Same root.)
palakh, subs. masc. sing cons. Ch. פְּלַח, "to worship."
pān, lit. "face," subs. masc. sing. Heb. פָּנֶה.
panū-a, or *panū-ya*, subs. sing. masc., with pron. suffix.
pani, lit. "before."
Pāppa, PAPHUS. Town on west coast of Cyprus.
parrati, subs. plu. fem. Heb. פָּרָה.
parikte, subs. fem. abs. Heb. פֶּרֶק.
pāskīs, adv. from *pasaku*.
pāsku, "difficult, broken." √ פשק. Chald. פְּסַק.
pattu, subs. sing. masc. Heb. פָּתַח.
pi, lit. "mouth." Heb. פֶּה.
pikhatu, subs. masc. Comp. Heb. פַּחָה.
pikhuti, subs. plu. of *pikhatu*.
pikitti, for *pikidti*, subs. sing. fem. Heb. פָּקַד.
pīli, subs. masc. sing.
pukhru, subs. sing. masc.  = *pu-ukh-ru* (ii. 2, 398).
Purrat. The river Euphrates. Heb. פְּרָת.
pukuttu. Comp. Heb. פָּקַע.

R

rabi, adj. plur. masc. Heb. רַב.
racbu, subs. sing. masc. Heb. רָכַב, "to ride."
rāhimat, subs. fem. sing. Heb. רָחַם.
ramani, reflex pron. "Excellently explained by Dr. Oppert. He first pointed out its true meaning and its derivation" (Sayce). Heb. רחם.
rarubat, "terror." It is thus translated generally. Prof. Sayce thinks the word is *rasubbat* (רשף), "the fire."
remu, subs. sing. masc. Comp. Heb. רַחֲמִים (Isa. xlvii. 6).
ribit, subs. plu. cons. Comp. Heb. רְחֹבוֹת. (For the Accad. equivalent see iv. 22, 20, and iv. 16, 52.)
ridūt, subs. fem. abs. Heb. רָדָה, "to rule over."
rimanis, adv. from *rimu*, "wild bull." Heb. רְאֵם.
rimi, lit. "the horned bull." It is also phonetically spelt .
risti, fem., from *risu*. Heb. רֵאשִׁית.
ritti, subs. fem. gen. case. Heb. רָדָה.
ritsuti, subs. fem. sing. Heb. רָצָה.
rucubi, subs. plu. masc. Heb. רֶכֶב.
rūku, adj. An interesting example of the loss of the ח. Heb. רָחַק.

S

sa, rel. pron. Identical with the later Heb. שֶׁ in Canticles, Judges and Ecclesiastes.
saladu, "length," as opposed to *rapastu*, "width."
sadi, subs. plu. masc. of *sadu*,  (iii. 70, 117). Arab. *saddun*, "mons."
saldhanis, adv. from *sildhanu*. Heb. שָׁלַט.

salgu, subs. sing. masc. nom. case. Heb. שֶׁלֶג .

salil, subs. masc. sing. cons. Heb. שָׁלָל .

sal-lamas's'i, subs. plu. masc. The ideograph is explained by *la-mas'-s'u* (ii. 1, 174). Prof. Sayce gives the rabbinic למס, as connected; the word is of Accadian origin (*Lectures*, p. 157). They are evidently of the same class of collossi that are to be seen in the British Museum.

sallat, subs. fem. sing. Heb. סָלַל, "to elevate."

Samsu. The Sun-god. Heb. שֶׁמֶשׁ . The sun has been deified by Eastern nations generally, and his power was looked upon as being considerable. He was supposed to be able to heal maladies (iv. 17). His title is generally "the judge of heaven and earth" (i. 9, 7), and "the Sun, the lady of the world" (iv. 32, 8). The month Tisri was dedicated to the "Sun-god, the warrior of the world." Its gender was feminine, but exceptions occur where the Sun is regarded as masculine, as in the Bible (Psalm civ. 19).

Samas-ibni. "The Sun-god created (me)."

samma, subs. masc. sing. accus. Heb. שׁוּם .

samna. Card. number. Heb. שְׁמֹנָה . *samna* is made fem. here, according to the custom of the Semetic languages, which is to use a fem. numeral before the masc. gender. Compare אַרְבָּעָה מְלָכִים, "four kings" (Gen. xiv. 9), and see the remarks on p. 221, of Roediger's *Grammar*, 21st edit.

Sams'imuruna. Biblical שֹׁמְרוֹן .

sanat, with prefix, "man of the year." Heb. שָׁנָה .

s'ānguti, sing. fem. abs., *sangu* = *magiru.* (ii. 27, 41). Assyrian √ מגר, "to be obedient."

sanna. Heb. שָׁנָה .

sanuvva, adj. with mimmation. Heb. שָׁנָה .

s'apinu, partic. Kal. Heb. סָפָה .

sar, cons. form of *saru.* Heb. שַׂר .

sarcu, adj. agreeing with *damū*, "white race," as opposed to *adamatu*, "black *or* red race."

sarruti, subs. fem. sing. Heb. שָׂרָה .

sāsu, demons. pron.

sasunu, demons. pron. plu. masc.

satti, for *santi*. Heb. שָׁנָה.

Sebatti. The month equivalent to our January. Heb. שְׁבָט. The ideograph for this month is .

sebie, subs. plu. Heb. שְׁבָצ.

secibu, partic. Kal. Heb. שָׁכַב.

sedi, subs. plu. masc. Explained by *se-e-du* (ii. 1, 174). Heb. שֵׁד; and see Deut. xxxii. 17.

SE-GA, "happy."  = *ma-ga-ru* (ii. 7, 28).  forms adjectives in Accadian.

selapis, adv. from *selapu*, "a fox;" and see the remarks under שועל in Gesenius' *Dict.*

sellulat. Comp. Heb. סֻלָּם.

sepā, subs. masc. dual., like *enā*, "eyes," *uzna*, "ears."

seri, subs. plu. Heb. שְׁאֵר.

sibittu. Comp. Heb. שִׁבְעָה.

s'iccat, subs. plu. fem. cons. Heb. סָכָךְ.

sicni. Comp. Heb. שָׁכֵן.

sidhir, subs. sing. masc. cons. Heb. שֹׁטֵר.

siellulat. See under *selullat*.

s'igar, subs. fem. cons. Comp. Heb. סגר.

sikhirti, "extent."

silasā. Comp. Heb. שְׁלֹשִׁים.

silate, subs. fem. Comp. Heb. שָׁלֵו, "tranquillity."

S'īllu, *Soloi*, *Soli* or *Sŏlŏe*. A seaport on the west part of north coast of Cyprus.

Sīluahme, *Salamis*, Σαλαμίς. A city at the east end of the island of Cyprus, not far from modern Famagosta.

SIM, subs. plur. Perhaps to be connected with שׁוּם, "a plant giving forth powerful odours."

simtu, subs. fem. sing. Heb. שָׁמַם.

SIN. "The Moon-god." His Accad. names were  A-CU (ii. 48, 48), and , EN-ZU, which is compounded in the name of Sennacherib (Bellino Cylinder, i.).

Contrary to the usage of the Western nations, the gender of the Moon-god was masculine, which is shown by the following line from iv. 33, 38:—"The month Sivan (dedicated) to the Moon-god, eldest son of Bel." The cult of the Moon-god was principally carried out in the city Ur. The wife of the Moon-god was called Nana (*La Magie*, 115). The daughter of the Moon-god was called Istar (iv. 31, 2).

Sin-akhi-irba, i.e., "Sin increases brothers."

s'iparru, subs. sing. masc. This ideograph is explained by *s'i-par-ru* (i. 1, 112, and see ii. 40, 48).

sitcin, subs. sing. masc., Iphteal deriv. Heb. שָׁכַן.

sit-cu-nu, 3rd plu. permans. Iphteal. Heb. שָׁכַן.

situte, subs. fem. plu.

subat-s'u, for *subat-su*, subs. fem. sing. Heb. יָשַׁב, "to dwell."

subtu, subs. fem sing. (Same root.)

sucun, imper. 2nd sing. masc., imper. Kal.

suklul. Shaphel deriv. Heb. כָּלַל.

sulmu, subs. sing. masc. Heb. שָׁלוֹם.

sum, subs. sing. masc. cons. Heb. שֵׁם.

sumelu, adj. Heb. שְׂמֹאל.

supar-saki. Conjectural reading, *supar*, means "over;" *sak*, Accad. deriv. = chief; hence, "man over my officers."

supul, subs. sing. cons. Comp. Heb. שְׁפֵלָה.

surman, subs. sing. masc. Comp. Syr. שורבינא, *pinus*, "pine tree." "Hoc *shar-bin* Arabicus prophetarum interpres ponit pro κυπάρισσος, Isai. xxxvii. 24 (Castell, *Lex*, p. 937).

surrute, subs. fem. plur. Heb. שָׂרָה, "to fight."

s'us'i, lit. "the animal from the east." Heb. סוּס.

sussu. Comp. Heb. שִׁשִּׁים.

sutesur, lit. "setting straight." Istaphal deriv. Heb. יָשַׁר, "to be straight."

T

takhatsi, for *tamkhatsi*. Tiphel deriv. from *makhatsu*. Heb. מְחַץ.

takhlupi, Tiphel deriv., subs. sing. masc. חָלַף, "to cover."

tallacti, subs. plur. fem. Tiphel deriv. Comp. Heb. הָלַךְ.

tamarti, subs. plur. √ אמר.

Tametsi. The Tămassus of classical authors; in the middle of Cyprus, 29 miles S.E. of Soloë (Smith, *Class. Dict.*).

tamsil. Tiphel deriv. Heb. מָשָׁל, "similitude."

tamtiv, subs. sing. fem. gen. case, with mimmation. Heb. תְּהוֹם.

tapdhūr, 3rd sing. fem. aor. Kal. Heb. פָּטַר.

tarbit, fem. abs. sing. Tiphel deriv. Heb. רָבָה.

Tarkū, Tirhakah. Biblical תִּרְהָקָה. Τεάρκων of Strabo, Τάρκος, or Ταρακός of Manetho.

tartsi, subs. masc. sing.

tasbir, 3rd sing. fem. aor. Kal. Heb. שָׁבַר.

tazīz, 3rd sing. fem. aor. Kal. √ זוז.

Tel-Assuri. Occurs in the form of *Telassar* (Isai. xxxvii. 12). Thus—תְּלַאשָּׂר.

tib. Tiphel deriv. cons. Heb. בּוֹא.

TIMMA, "rope, cable." See Syl. No. 93.

timme, subs. masc. sing.

tsabi, subs. plu. masc. Heb. צָבָא.

tsabi-mitpani, i.e., "bowmen."

tsakhra, adj. sing. Heb. צָעִיר.

tsakhri, adj. masc. (Same root.)  = *tsa-akh-ru* (ii. 48, 20).

tsatsāte, subs. masc. sing., "image or statuary work." Comp. Heb. צַעֲצֻעִים (2 Chron. iii. 10.)

tsidit, subs. plu. fem. Heb. צֵידָה (Gen. xlii. 25).

Tsidunni. The Phœnician "fishing" city. Heb. צִידוֹן.

tseni, subs. plu. masc. Heb. צֹאן.

tsimitti. Comp. Heb. צֶמֶד.

tsipri, subs. masc. sing. gen. case. Heb. צָבַר, "to heap up."
TSIR, from Accad.
tsirūssu, for *tsiru-su*, prep. with enclitic pron.
tsit, fem. abs. Heb. יָצָא, "to go forth."
tsūbbubu, subs. plu. Heb. צָב (Levit. xi. 29).
tsumami, subs. masc. gen. case. Heb. צָמָא, "thirst;" used of thirsty (*i.e.*, desert) land, Isai. xliv. 3. Similar forms are *samami*, "heavens," *mami*, "waters."
Tsurri. Biblical צוֹר; Aram. טְרָא; Greek Τύρος.
tsutsi, subs. masc. plu. of *tsutsu*. Heb. צִיץ, "a flower."
tugulti, fem. abs. sing.
tulā, subs. sing. masc. accus. case. Heb. תֵּל.

U

u. Heb. וְ, "and." Note the frequent use in this inscription of  instead of .
ucci, 1st sing. masc. aor. Kal, for *unci*. Heb. נָכָה.
ucin, 1st sing. aor. Aphel. Heb. כּוּן.
ucni, subs. masc. sing. gen. case. It is called . Heb. יָפֶה, which proves it to have been a *white* stone of some sort (*Trans. Soc. Bib. Arch.*, vol. vi.: *Les noms de l'Airain*, etc.).
udannin, 1st pers. sing. aor. Pael, from √ *dananu*, "to be strong."
uddis, 1st sing. aor. Pael of *khadasu*, "to be new." Heb. חָדַשׁ.
Udume. Biblical אֱדוֹם. New Test. 'Εδώμ.
uduri, subs. plu. masc. Heb. עֵדֶר.
ugaru (*agar*), subs. masc. sing. A syllabary makes *ugaru* = *agar*. Its numbers are K 4403, K 4319, K 4604, ⊕ 279.
ukhallik, 1st pers. sing. aor. Pael. Heb. חָלַק, "to despoil" (2 Chron. xxviii. 21).
ulluti, prep. A curious compound of this word with *anacu* occurs in i. 59, 55, *ul-la-nu-cu*, "I am from ancient times."

ultu, prep. Prof. Sayce compares Ethiopic "*wĕsta*" (*Lectures*, p. 105).

ummanu, subs. plu. masc. Heb. הָמוֹן, lit. "many soldiers."  (ii. 2, 293); Heb. צָבָא.  (i. 21, 64); Heb. מְאֹד.

ummi, lit. "mothers," plu. fem. of *ummu*. Heb. אֵם.

unammera, 1st pers. sing. obj. aor. Pael.

unute, subs. fem. plu. Heb. הוֹן.

upakhir, 1st pers. sing. aor. Pael. √ בחר.

urā, 1st sing. obj. aor. Kal. Heb. יָרָה.

urabbi, 1st pers. sing. masc. aor. Pael. Heb. רָבָה.

uraccis', 1st pers. sing. aor. Pael. Heb. רָכַס.

uraddi, 1st sing. aor. Pael.

urās's'iba, 1st pers. sing. obj. aor. Pael. Arab. *rashaba*.

usāski, 1st sing. aor. Shaphel. Heb. שָׁקָה.

usassi sunuti, 1st sing. aor. Shaphel. נָשָׂא, with plu. masc. pron.

urattā, 1st pers. aor. Pael. √ רתח.

urikhte. The word literally means "quick."

Uru. The Biblical אוּר of Gen. xi. 28. Now Mugheir. Χαλδαίων πόλις (Gesenius).

urrūkhis, adv. "quickly."

usaclil, 1st sing. aor. Shaphel. Heb. כָּלַל.

usadgil, 1st sing. aor. Shaphel. √ דגל.

usakhbiba, 1st pers. sing. aor. Shaphel.

usaldidūni, 3rd plu. perf. Shaphel. √ שרד.

usalizu, 1st sing. aor. Shaphel. Heb. עלז.

usalmā, 1st sing. masc. obj. aor. Kal. Chald. שְׁלָם, "to complete."

usarkhits, 1st sing. masc. aor. Shaphel. רָחַץ.

us'arrid, 1st sing. masc. aor. Shaphel. Heb. יָרַד.

usāsdhir, 1st sing. aor. Shaphel. Heb. שָׁטַר.

usās'khira, 1st sing. masc. aor. Shaphel. Heb. סָחַר.

usatritsa, 1st sing. aor. Shaphel. √ תרץ.

usatsbat, 1st sing. masc. pres. Shaphel. Arab. *tsabata*.

usatsbita, 1st sing. masc. pres. Shaphel.

useli-suva, 1st pers. sing. aor. Shaphel. Heb. עָלָה, with pers. pron. *su* and enclitic *va*.
usemid, 1st sing. aor. Shaphel. Heb. עָמַד.
usepis, 1st sing. masc. aor. Shaphel. √ עבש, *episu* = *banu*, "to make" (ii. 60, 41).
useserav-va, 1st sing. aor. Shaphel. Heb. יָשַׁר, and enclitic *va*.
usesib, 1st sing. aor. Shaphel. Heb. יָשַׁב.
usmalli, 1st sing. aor. Shaphel. Heb. מָלֵא.
ussi, subs. fem. sing. Heb. אֲשִׁישׁ.
utir, 1st sing. aor. Aphel. Heb. תּוּר.
uzain, 1st sing. aor. Kal. Comp. Aram. זין.
uzna, subs. dual. Heb. אָזְנַיִם.

V

va, conjunction. Heb. וְ.

Y

Yâtnana. Cyprus. The usual name for the island of Cyprus in the cuneiform inscriptions. It was situated, according to *W.A.I.* (iii. 11, 29), *malac* vii. *yumi ina kabal tamti erib Samsi*, "a journey of seven days in the middle of the sea of the setting sun" (*i.e.*, Mediterranean).
yaudi. Biblical יְהוּדָה.
yubil, 3rd sing. aor. Aphel. Heb. בָּלָה. Used of a man who through sickness wastes away.
yucin, 3rd sing. masc. aor. Aph. כּוּן.
yumas's'aru, 3rd plu. masc. aor. Pael. Heb. מָסַר.
yumas's'ir, 3rd sing. masc. aor. Pael.
yumi, subs. plu. of *yumu*. Heb. יוֹם.
yunaccir, 3rd sing. masc. aor. Pael.
yunassik, 3rd sing. masc. aor. Pael. Heb. נָשַׁק.
yupalladh, 3rd sing. masc. aor. Pael. פָּלַט in Hiphil, "to deliver from danger."

yuracsa, 3rd sing. masc. obj. aor. Kal. Heb. רָכַם.

yusezibu, 3rd sing. masc. aor. Kal. √ עזב.

yusesibuni, 3rd plu. masc. perf. Heb. יָשַׁב.

yutarru, 3rd plu. masc. aor. Pael. Heb. תּוּר.

yutir, 3rd sing. masc. aor. Aph.; and see Sayce, *Grammar* (Bagster), p. 63.

yutsallani, 3rd sing. masc. obj. aor. Pael, with poss. pron. suffix *ni*. Chald. צְלָא.

Z

zicari. Comp. Heb. זְכַר.

zicir, subs. sing. masc. Heb. זֶכֶר. For the use of this word for "name," see Exod. iii. 15.

zirbabi, subs. plu. masc.

INDEX.

THE END.

PRINTED BY BALLANTYNE AND HANSON
LONDON AND EDINBURGH

www.ingramcontent.com/pod-product-compliance
Lightning Source LLC
Chambersburg PA
CBHW032155160426
43197CB00008B/929
* 9 7 8 3 3 3 7 2 4 5 8 0 1 *